# THE BEAUTIFUL GAME

## THE MOST AMAZING FOOTBALL STORIES OF ALL TIME

MICHAEL LANGDON

"Some people believe football is a matter of life and death, I am very disappointed with that attitude. I can assure you it is much, much more important than that."

Bill Shankly 1913–1981

*For my nearest and dearest.*

*Those (un)lucky enough to be touched by,*

*and have suffered the consequences of,*

*my irrational love for football.*

*I dedicate this book to you with all my love.*

# CONTENTS

# INTRODUCTION

For over 150 years, billions of people from every corner of the world have been transfixed by football's tales of wonder.

Stories of passion and love, of sadness and tragedy. Stories that unite all football fans across the world in a common love for the game. The kind of love that gives us all a bit of joy and escapism.

Sit back, and enjoy 90 of the best stories that this beautiful game has given us.

# CHAPTER 1
# WHEN THINGS SPILL OVER

# THE FOOTBALL WAR

Football is a game of passion – a passion so strong that it regrettably spills over at times.

In 1969, tensions were running high between El Salvador and Honduras. During the summer the countries clashed over many political issues like immigration, agriculture, and land-reform policies.

That summer also saw the football-mad latino nations involved in two play-off games to decide who would go to the 1970 World Cup. Stakes could not get any higher.

They played the two games with a victory for each team - nothing could separate them, so the fixture had to go to a deciding third game in Mexico City.

On the day of that deciding football game, El Salvador dissolved all diplomatic ties with Honduras, accusing them of murder, oppression and rape. The opposing fans inside the stadium, undoubtedly fuelled by their governments' actions, started scuffles and fights in the stands.

El Salvador won that deciding game and ended up going to the World Cup in Mexico - those fans fighting in the stands *could surely not* expect what was about to come...

Two weeks later, and from tensions still boiling from the recent football games, El Salvador invaded its neighbouring country.

It sent its airforce to bomb Honduran airstrips in an effort to stun their military forces. It was also hoping to nullify any potential aerial counterattack. War broke out.

The war lasted four days (it's referred to as "the hundred hour war" in some places), but it still killed approximately 3,000 people. The Organisation of American States (OAS) quickly intervened to stop more bloodshed.

Although it would be very naive (and factually incorrect) to solely blame a game of football for the 100 hour war, those three games certainly played a big role in stoking the fire between those two nations before they went to war.

It is one of the most extreme and vivid examples in history of football passion taking over with such irrational and deadly outcomes.

This, of course, is not the only extraordinary act that football has caused when emotions take over.

Sometimes, they are slightly more bizarre, and occur under an even bigger spotlight…

# A HEADBUTT TO HONOUR
# HIS SISTER

Football greatness is very subjective. In deciding who the best player to *ever* play the game is, the experts will likely mention one of four: Pelé, Maradona, Ronaldo and Messi.

The one thing the connoisseurs will *objectively* agree on though, is which of the world greats had the most incredible last game of their career.

It is a story that defies belief. A story so outrageous that even the most creative of Hollywood script writers could not get close to concocting the events that took place in Berlin's Olympiastadion on the evening of July 9th 2006.

The biggest game in world football, the World Cup final, comes round once every four years. One seventh of all humanity watches the game live.

In 2006, and with a billion eyes watching him, Zinedine Zidane decided to score one of the most audacious goals ever seen in a World Cup final. A 'Panenka' penalty kick (a cheeky and unexpected dink of the ball that only the bravest of footballers ever dare to think about, let alone execute).

That would be reason to celebrate the occasion. An occasion when this legend of the game (and previous world cup winner) was playing his last ever match as a professional.

However, it is what happened 100 minutes later that has gone down as the stuff of football folklore.

With Italy and France tied at 1-1, and with the game inevitably going to penalties to decide who the winner of football's most coveted prize would be, Italian defender Marco Materazzi and Zinedine Zidane had a coming together on the pitch. Nothing unusual - just part of the game.

As is often the case in football, less talented players seek out the shirts of more talented players to keep as sporting mementos. Zidane, in an attempt to wind up Materazzi said to the defender after the scuffle: 'I'll give you my shirt later'. Zidane was implying to Materazzi that he was a superior football player to him (which, to be perfectly frank, he was).

Materazzi replied: "I'd rather have your sister than your shirt."

In what can only be described as the biggest "red-rag-to-a-bull" moment in football history, Zidane threw himself, head-first, into the chest of Materazzi. The referee missed the incident, but the assistant referee didn't. After a private chat between the two, the referee had no option but to send him off minutes before the penalty shootout.

In a game where he had *already* scored a penalty.

That infamous headbutt cost France the chance to become world champions in 2006. It also robbed the world of a dignified fairytale ending to one of the world's best football players.

# MORE RED CARDS THAN PLAYERS ON THE PITCH

Having a player sent off during a game of football can be very detrimental for a team (Just ask Zidane's 2006 team-mate Willy Sagnol who didn't speak to the French forward for two years after that infamous headbutt).

But when 36 people are sent off in a game it's just utter chaos.

In 2011, Argentinian fifth tier outfit Claypole played bitter rivals Victoriano Arenas. It was a fiery affair, with the only thing of note being the two red cards shown to each team just before half time.

The second half saw Claypole score twice and secure a 2-0 victory.

It was *after* the full time whistle that this particular game of football quickly turned into a raucous MMA arena.

The mother of all fights broke out in the centre circle. And it wasn't just the players on the pitch getting involved. Not wanting to be left out, along came the substitutes and the coaching staff of both teams to throw some punches around. Legend has it that even the coach drivers of the opposing teams got involved in the action!

In the aftermath of the storm, referee Damian Rubino walked into the dressing room of both teams to individually send off every single member of staff in each team.

That amounted to 36 red cards in total, and a Guinness Book of World Records award for the most sendings off in a single game of football!

# DRAWING BLOOD AT THE MARACANA

Despite the scuffles between Claypole and Victoriano Arenas players in 2011, there was definitely no blood spilled on the pitch.

That cannot be said about a 1989 World Cup qualifying game between Brazil and Chile, where one of the most brazen and infamous attempts at cheating took place.

Chile were losing 1-0 and needed a win to qualify for the World Cup Finals. It was the 70th minute and they were quickly running out of time.

Out of nowhere, a flare was thrown onto the pitch, landing very close to the Chilean goalkeeper.

As people turned around to see what the commotion was, they saw the Chilean goalkeeper, Roberto Rojas, writhing and clutching his head. There was blood pouring from his forehead.

Chile's captain ordered his players to go back into the changing rooms and not to come out. He cited a lack of safety for his players as the reason to abstain from playing. The match was abandoned.

Chile was hoping for FIFA to punish Brazil by awarding the victory to Chile. In what can only be described as the perfect example of divine justice, the exact opposite happened.

After a careful investigation, FIFA awarded Brazil a 2-0 victory and banned Chile from the 1994 World Cup.

What transpired after a careful review of footage and images from the game is one of the most bizarre things to have ever happened on a football pitch.

Roberto Rojas had hidden a razor in his gloves. When the flare was thrown close to him onto the pitch, he made the most of that opportunity.

Whilst clutching his head, he pulled out the razor from within his glove. He then cut himself deeply in the forehead so that he'd bleed profusely and be seen as *obviously* having an injury. He was taken off on a stretcher to make it more believable.

This 'Plan B' approach to winning a game has never been seen before. And probably for good reason.

FIFA gave Roberto Rojas a lifetime ban from playing the sport and the man now walks around with a scar on his forehead to remind him of his shameful act.

# CHAPTER 2
## FOOTLOL TALES

# THE SMELL OF DISASTER

The beautiful game has provided many funny tales. Whilst some of them are laugh out loud funny, others are peculiar.

Santiago Cañizares of Spain starred in one such tale in 2002. A story many found peculiar, but one that Cañizares himself certainly did NOT find funny.

The Spaniards were going through a football renaissance, and entered the tournament as one of the favourites.

Cañizares had just established himself as the Spanish number one goalkeeper, which at 32 years old, was some-what late. The goalkeeper must have been feeling buoyant heading into that particular weekend. It was the weekend before the flight to Japan and the 2002 World Cup, where he'd be representing his country at the pinnacle of his sporting career.

Whilst in his hotel room, he headed into the bathroom to prepare himself for the night - that's when disaster struck!

His teammates heard a commotion from across the hall, and wanting to find out what had happened, they rushed to Cañizares' room only to be stopped by the doctors.

"Don't come in - there's glass everywhere" Doctors told his teammates.

Fearing the worst (break-in, suicide, intruder) his teammates were somewhat relieved a few minutes later when they heard the news from the doctors.

It turned out that Cañizares accidentally knocked over a bottle of aftershave that was sitting on the bathroom sink. The bottle smashed on the floor and broke into lots of tiny pieces and a couple of large shards.

Unfortunately for Spain's number one, one of those large shards flew into his right foot and severed his tendon. He missed the World Cup and was out of action for a month.

Incidentally, that incident propelled Iker Casillas to become Spain's main goalkeeper. A role he secured for a number of years, and which saw him become a World Cup winning captain in 2010.

You could say Cañizares' injury was a 'god-scent' of an occurrence for Casillas.

# THE PSYCHIC OCTOPUS

Despite being a World Cup winner that year, Iker Casillas wasn't the star of the show in South Africa in 2010. It wasn't even a footballer who stole the show, it was a psychic invertebrate!

When it comes to divination, there are many different methods that people use in order to try and predict the future. Some use tarot cards, others palm reading, some even do tea leaves.

One of the most unusual methods is using an octopus.

Paul the psychic octopus became famous for his ability to correctly predict the outcomes of football matches, including the 2010 World Cup final match which saw Spain become champions.

So how did he do it? Paul, who resided in a tank in Germany, would be fed from two boxes that were draped in the flags of the countries that were playing a match that day.

Whichever box he opened first would be deemed as his prediction as to which country would win the game.

In July 2010 Germany were playing Spain in the semi-final of the World Cup. That morning, Paul chose to have his breakfast from a box draped in a Spanish flag instead of the one draped in the German flag - he broke millions of German hearts that morning.

Lo and behold, and as foretold by one of the greatest psychics the world has ever seen, Germany went on to lose the semi-final 1-0.

Paul had a 100% success rate in guessing correct predictions during that world cup. Arguably the finest performance of 2010 and without a doubt winning the hearts of millions of football fans on every continent on earth.

After taking some time off from the limelight, Paul Sadly passed away a few months after the world cup. He took the Rainbow Bridge to Octopus Heaven on October 26th 2010.

# LYING ABOUT YOUR GRANDMOTHER'S DEATH... TWICE!

It would be remiss to talk about Rainbow Bridges walks without mentioning Stephen Ireland's grandmother. Both his paternal *and* maternal one, who were killed off by the Irish player in order to get out of playing for Ireland.

I mean, we've all been there, right? There's something you *have* to do but you really don't want to do it.

99% of people would not classify playing football for your country as a chore, but then again, Stephen Ireland was different class.

In 2007, when he was called up for an international football match, he claimed he was sick. The problem was that the Irish manager had just seen him put on a Man of the Match performance for Manchester City live on TV.

He decided to tell a little white lie and claim that his grandmother Patricia Tallon had died. And that he needed time to grieve.

That was all well and good until Patricia read about her own death in the national newspaper and rebutted the claim! She argued that had she indeed been dead, she wouldn't be able to read the article. Very few people could argue against her case.

Ireland then said it was his paternal grandmother that had died. Something that Brenda Kitchener (his paternal grandmother) wasn't too happy about when *she* read about her own death in the national newspaper! Perhaps lacking a bit of creativity, she used the same defence as Patricia when explaining that it was impossible for her to be dead.

Ireland then went on to claim that it was actually his divorced grandfather's partner that had died, before realising that people who are alive can quite easily prove that they are not dead. (what's that about footballers not being the sharpest tools in the shed?!)

Ireland had become entangled in such a large web of deceit that he had to come clean in the end.

His girlfriend had suffered a miscarriage and he wanted to spend some time with her during that difficult time.

Ireland's international career never recovered after that incident - he represented his country a meagre six times (not enough for someone of his talent).

Some would argue that his club career never recovered from that incident either. Having once been voted Manchester City's player of the year, he fell into relative football obscurity until his retirement in 2018.

Moral of the story for the young ones out there: Honesty is *always* the best policy.

# THAT'S JUST SCILLY - THE WORLD'S SMALLEST FOOTBALL LEAGUE

From Stephen Ireland's silly antics we move to Scilly's football ladder.

The Scilly Isles are an archipelago off the Cornish Coast, in southwest England. With a population of just over two thousand people, the Scilly Isles doesn't seem like the most likely place for a football league. But against all odds, there is in fact a Scilly Isles football league - boasting an impressive two teams!

And while the football might not be of the same standard as the Premier League, the Scilly Isles football league offers its own brand of charm - even if it lacks a little excitement.

The league competition involves the Woolpack Wanderers and the Garrison Gunners playing each other 18 times throughout the season.

The beauty of this league is that you're poised for success if you're lucky enough to play for one of these two teams, with the odds always being 50/50 that you'll end up being champions of Scilly.

Games are often on a Sunday, and much like Inter Milan vs AC Milan derbies at the San Siro, both teams in Scilly are always playing at home in the St Mary's Island local pitch.

Another perk of playing football in the Scilly Isles, is that if at any time one of the teams is running away with the league (Woolpack Wanderers are, at the time of writing, smashing the opposition) then there are always cup competitions to look forward to.

Two domestic cup competitions (The Wholesalers Cup and the Foredeck Cup) also take place in Scilly, and the long and arduous route to the final is always contested by the same two teams.

On top of the two cup competitions and a gruelling league competition that goes from Mid November to the end of March, the football association of Scilly also puts on a Charity Shield competition as the season's curtain raiser.

And the two teams to compete in the Charity Shield? You guessed it. Woolpack Wanderers and the Garrison Gunners.

A league with no relegation scraps and where bitter rivals go head to head every single weekend. Imagine if we got that with River Plate vs Boca Juniors or Fenerbahce and Galatasaray? The Scilly Isles footballers get a worthy mention in this book!

# HAVE A DIG!

From somewhat of a metaphorical graveyard league in Scilly, we move to a literal grave dug in Acarigua, Venezuela in 1978.

A Copa Libertadores match between Cerro Porteno of Paraguay and Portuguesa of Venezuela ended in a dull 1-1 affair.

Colombian referee Orlando Sanchez blew his full time whistle and together with his assistants went back into the changing room to shower and head off to the airport to make their flights back home.

It was during their journey from Acarigua to Caracas, that their car was intercepted by Portuguesa fans and, at gunpoint, they were kicked and dragged out of the car.

They were pulled (by their hair!) to a waiting spade and told at gunpoint to dig their own grave.

Having already refereed a laborious 90 minutes, a terrified and desolate Sanchez had no option but to start digging.

As the referee dug what was destined to be his last resting place, he couldn't help but wonder exactly what decisions had made the local fans so angry. Apart from 2 goals, the game had been a rather nondescript affair.

Just as he had resigned himself to his life coming to an end in Caracas, a few police cars miraculously appeared on the scene and saved his life.

Where they came from, he does not know, but the eternally grateful referee continued on his journey to the airport and flew back to Colombia - never to set foot on Venezuelan soil ever again!

Portuguesa were fined $5,000 and banned from playing in their stadium for a year.

If ever a referee has a bad game, they'd do well to remember that at least they were not minutes from dying in a self-dug shallow grave.

# ABSOLUTELY DENTAL!

From one refereeing nightmare to another. And unfortunately for Danish side Ebeltoft, they were the victims of a howler by referee Henning Erikstrup.

Picture the scene: Norager are playing Ebeltoft. It's a 4-3 thriller of a game and it's getting to the 90th minute.

Given the high scoring nature of the game already, anything is possible. Ebeltoft players can smell blood - their opponents are nervous. They go on one last attack.

As this last attack unfolds, and running at the same pace of the attacking side, referee Erikstrup puts his whistle to his lips to blow for full time.

This seemingly uncomplicated manoeuvre goes as bad as it possibly can and his dentures fly out of his mouth. The momentum of the attack means that the referee now finds himself a few dozen yards away from his teeth. And no teeth means no final whistle .

As the referee runs back to collect his teeth, play continues and Ebeltoft score a last-gasp equaliser to make it 4-4. Wild scenes ensue. The comeback of all comebacks. The resilience and grit shown by the players of Ebeltoft was nothing short of remarkable.

Unfortunately it's about to be taken away from them. After a couple of minutes of wild celebrations, the referee blows his whistle to disallow the last minute equaliser.

In the most brazen act of shamelessness, and showing no sign of self-dignity (and too much respect to the laws of the game), he goes on to the explain to the enraged Ebeltoft players that the goal does not stand because he tried to blow for full time as the attack was unfolding. He just could not do it because he had lost his dentures.

Any person with half an ounce of shame and common sense would have let the goal stand and casually pick their dentures up from the centre circle without anyone noticing.

Perhaps, if caught and under remonstration, say that his lack of teeth was most certainly *not* the reason why he hadn't blown for full time. That he was just letting the game flow.

But no. Not Henning Erikstrup. Not this stickler for the rules. The Dane had no problems in highlighting his embarrassing mishap in order to honour the rules of the game!

Ebeltoft protested against the result to the Danish FA - but the country's football association stuck by their referee and Norager kept their win.

# NOT TOO XAVI A DREAM

In July 2005 a Liverpool fan by the name of Adrian Hayward went to sleep just like he did any other night.

Perhaps still buoyed by his team's recent comeback in the Champions League Final in Istanbul (more on the greatest comeback in footballing history in Chapter 6), he had Liverpool FC on his mind.

That night he dreamt that Liverpool's Xabi Alonso scored a goal from his own half. And what does any reasonable person do after they dream of a sporting achievement? Well, they go down to the local bookmakers to place a bet on that dream becoming a reality.

So off he went to his local bookmaker and put a £200 bet on Xavi Alonso scoring from his own half that season. The odds were 125-1.

Paddy Power (his local bookmaker) thought it was the easiest £200 they had ever made!

But 6 months later, on a rainy day in Luton, England, Adrian Hayward's dream became a reality.

Liverpool were playing Luton away in the FA CUP. They were 4-3 up in the 90th minute when Luton got a corner kick.

With nothing to lose, Luton sent everyone into the opposition's box for that last corner kick (goalkeeper included). The Liverpool defenders managed to half clear the ball and it fell to the feet of Xabi Alonso. Alonso was in his own half but knew the opposing keeper was nowhere near his goal.

So what is a man to do but try his luck? (and Adrian Hayward's for that matter).

Xabi pinged a 70-yard shot from well within his half, and it slowly trickled (it must have been the most agonising wait for Hayward) into the opposition's net.

That goal sealed Liverpool's passage into the next round and it also made Adrian Hayward £25,000 richer.

Paddy Power was later quoted as saying: "It's great when these unusual bets pay out".

We don't believe they meant a word of it.

# A FLYING HEADER

"Flying headers" are scored all the time in football. That is the metaphorical term that football pundits and fanatics use when a player leaps in the air and makes contact with the football using their head.

As far as we are aware, there is only one *literal* flying header to have ever been scored in a game of football. And that accolade goes to an unknown seagull in Manchester, England.

At the beginning of the 1999 season, Stalybridge Celtic Colts were playing Hollingworth Juniors in a local amateur league in the north of England.

It was a low-league encounter in a schoolboys match, so the footballing standards weren't very high.

As a matter of fact, the expectations were so low that when 13-year-old striker Danny Worthington volleyed a shot towards goal no one batted an eyelid. The ball looked like it was destined for Row Z (if the kids were to play in a stadium).

It was as the ball's trajectory kept sailing skyward that one of the most unusual things ever seen on a football field was witnessed.

Bear in mind that, by this point, Danny had already turned away in disgust at how rubbish his attempt on goal had been.

Shoulders slumped, he was about to apologise to his team-mates for a pathetic excuse of a shot, when they all started running towards him in ecstasy. They were celebrating a goal!

Tuning back to find the ball in the back of the net, Danny put his arms in the air in evident self-praise. He had no idea how the ball had ended up there, but that wasn't going to stop him from celebrating!

In hindsight, it was a bit of an overzealous celebration for an assist.

That's right, Danny got credited with an assist and the official goal went to a hapless seagull that was flying over the penalty spot.

Unbeknownst to Danny, his looping shot hit the seagull as the bird was swooping down. The ball ricocheted off the bird and into the back of the net.

The bird fell to the ground for a few seconds before regaining consciousness and flying away into the horizon in celebration of its goal.

Legend has it that Alex Ferguson, the Manchester United boss at the time, was so impressed with this bird that it spurred him on to sign the likes of *Robin* Van Persie and Chris *Eagles*.

# MAKING A DOG'S DINNER OUT OF IT

You could be forgiven for thinking that birds were the only animals to score on the football pitch. However, there are countless tales of man's best friend getting on the scoresheet.

The most famous of these occasions must be the goal scored for Deportivo San Miguel de Rio Viejo during a Chilean football game in 2021.

As San Miguel lined up to a free kick on the edge of the area, they called up their centre backs.

What the opposition (Real Zaragoza) didn't know was that they had a secret weapon up their sleeve.

As the free kick was taken, a (seemingly stray) alsatian cleverly beat the offside trap (although this is hotly disputed due to lack of VAR in Chilean amateur football) to head into the bottom left corner of the net - leaving Real Zaragoza's goalkeeper flat-footed and in no man's land.

It really was a goal that Didier Dogba or Terrier Henry would have been proud of.

A notable mention for another great pooch on a football field story must go to one of the greatest saves ever seen. One that would make even Peter Schmeichel be proud of. After all, he is the Great Dane!

The scene was Greater Glasgow, the playground of the footballing elite, and Vale of Leven AFC and Ferguslie Star were battling it out in the AFL President's Cup match. It was a winner-takes-all affair.

Vale of Leven ended up winning the game 3-2, so you can imagine how enraged Ferguslie striker Ross Hamilton was when he beat the offside trap, latched onto a long ball, and slotted past the keeper only to find his shot blocked by a dog having a good ol' sniff at the near post.

Annoyingly for Ferguslie Star, the ball rebounded off the dog and landed at the feet of one of their strikers who scored, but the referee ruled the goal out because of the dog's interference and gave the Leven goalkeeper a drop ball.

# TRIPLE WORD SORE

We started this chapter with one of the most ludicrous injuries in the history of our sport. And we will finish it with another.

Funnily enough, it happened to another goalkeeper. And no, this isn't the story of English international goalkeeper David Seaman getting injured as he stretched for the remote controller in bed (also a true story - what is it about goalkeepers and silly injuries?!).

Nor is it the story of promising Danish Liverpool goalkeeper Michael Stensgaard. As he was reaching out for the pull-down ironing board in his room, Stensgaard dislocated his shoulder. The promising goalkeeper was forced to retire through this injury.

This is the story of Lionel Letizi, and he takes the accolade for the world's most bizarre injury.

In 2002 The French goalkeeper injured his back whilst playing the very physical game of scrabble.

Yup, the very same game that great grandmothers around the world play in comfy sofas for hours on end.

As the French goalkeeper and wordsmith was preparing a sumptuous 50+ scoring word, a couple of tiles fell on the floor.

It was as he bent over to pick them up that he pulled some muscles in his back. He was out injured for quite some time and never really recovered to his previous best.

Some people questioned the veracity of his injury, insinuating he only made up the injury to get out of some commitments (A la Stephen Ireland perhaps?!). Those very people claimed the tiles he was reaching for were BS.

Two other honourable mentions for bizarre injuries must go to Darius Vasell of England, who tried to alleviate a blood blister in his toe by drilling through his toenail with an electric power drill and to midfielder Adam Chapman of Oxford United who had to go to hospital with a burnt nipple after spilling baby milk on his chest.

# CHAPTER 3
## SUPERHUMAN STORIES

# THE SCORPION KICK

Regulated football has been played for approximately 160 years. Because it's been that long, it is fair to say that nothing of novelty often happens on the football pitch.

Yes, it's an exciting sport, but most of the time, you know – to a reasonable extent – what is going to happen.

Colombian goalkeeper Rene Higuita didn't ever do ordinary, though.

He was an eccentric goalkeeper, often playing out of his area by taking on opposition strikers with the ball at his feet. A clear showman who, in an effort to give people thrills and entertainment, often disregarded his teammates' desire to win games.

He wanted to entertain people so much that he also pioneered the trend of goalkeepers scoring goals. The footballing world had rarely seen a goalkeeper who would take free kicks and penalties before Higuita made it vogue - scoring a healthy 41 goals in his career)

With a quality mullet to go with his vivacious attitude, and a personal life that left many wondering what he got up to in his private life (he was often photographed with drug barons, models and gangsters) he found himself in prison in 1993 after being involved in a kidnapping in Colombia.

Perhaps it was during his time behind bars that he perfected the move that would make him a global footballing legend.

On September 6 1995, Colombia were playing England in a game at the 'Home' of football, Wembley stadium in London.

During the game, Jamie Redknapp lobbed an aimless ball into the goalmouth - an easy catch for any goalkeeper.

"I could catch it safely…" Higuita probably thought. "Nah, screw that, let's go down in history!"

Instead of catching the ball (like anyone else would), the goalkeeper decided to lob himself in front of the ball, contort himself in mid air in the shape of a scorpion, and use his 'stinger' (his two legs arching over his back) to clear the ball out of his area.

The English football commentator of the game was obviously not expecting that - "Goodness me!" he shrieked.

The next day, in every playground in every country, school children across the world were trying this move themselves.

Never again has a keeper attempted this audacious move during a game.

Higuita was later quoted as saying that he wanted to entertain the fans as it was a dull 0-0 affair and he was hearing some boos from the stand.

It seems those boos were simply too much for this showman.

# A PAIN IN THE NECK

From one goalkeeping great to another. And Bert Trauttmann's life story is one of the most remarkable stories in world football.

Much like Higuita though, he will be remembered specifically for the events of one game.

Bert grew up in Germany and went through the Hitler Youth before joining the Nazi war efforts. During the war, he was captured by the allies and spent several years in England as a Prisoner of War.

It was at the detention camps that he caught the eye of football enthusiasts, as they had rarely seen a man so efficient inbetween the sticks.

After the war ended, he settled in England - finding a wife and starting a family. He made Manchester his home, and in doing so, became Manchester City's first team goalkeeper.

In the 1956 FA Cup final, Manchester City were playing Birmingham City at Wembley to decide the English Cup Champions.

With a quarter of an hour to play, a ball was played into City's box and a Birmingham striker nodded it down towards his oncoming teammate. His teammate would have slotted it into the back of the net had it not been for Bert Trautmann. Or to be more specific, Bert Trautmann's neck.

The momentum of the rushing striker carried him (knee first!) straight into Trautmann's neck, and whilst the keeper made the save, he lay motionless on the Wembley turf for a good few minutes.

He eventually got up whilst massaging his neck. A bit like when one sleeps at a funny angle and wakes up with a sore neck.

Trauttmann's neck wasn't sore. He had actually broken 5 vertebrae in his neck and came close to dying as one of those vertebrae actually split into two.

Luckily for Trauttmann, English treatment for broken necks in the 1950s was world class. The physio rushed onto the pitch and fixed the injury by rubbing a wet sponge all over the keeper's face.

That allowed Trauttmann to keep playing in the game - remarkably making a couple of great saves (one which included another collision with a striker) - and become an FA Cup winner.

He would go on to collect his winners medal (still clutching his neck as if he'd had a bad sleep) from the Royal Box.

It was only a few days later, after the pain was not subsiding, that he had his injury checked out and realised the severity of it. He went on to spend 5 months in a plaster that stretched from his hip to his head.

Trautmann could have easily died or been left paralysed that day. Instead he kept on playing and picked up a winner's medal. That gives him an honourable mention in this book!

# THE KAISER

Another superhuman story of grit and resilience through injury (or just pure madness?!) goes to Trautmann's compatriot and one of history's very best players, Franz Beckenbauer. Also known as "The Kaiser".

The German midfielder (who then went on to make a name for himself as a defender who pioneered the sweeper role) was one of the most elegant and reliable defensive players ever.

In a World Cup semi-final game in 1970 he had one of his most incredible games. The game was dubbed "The Game of Century" - purely because it was a 4-3 thriller between two stalwarts of the world game, Germany and Italy.

But on a personal level for Beckenbauer, what he did on the pitch that day defies belief.

After an early challenge by an Italian player, Beckenbauer landed awkwardly on his shoulder and broke his collarbone.

Any normal person would have gone straight to hospital, but not Der Kaiser.

Instead he ordered his medical team to bring a sling onto the pitch. He placed his broken clavicle into the sling and continued to play for not only 90 minutes, but a whole 120 minutes, with the game going to extra time before Italy snatched victory at the death.

Whilst Trautmann's injury was a lot worse, he was somewhat protected by his players when in between the goal. What makes Beckenbauer's performance so incredible is that he produced a *masterclass* of a display that day

In a world cup semi-final.

With a broken bone.

With one of his limbs strapped to his chest.

In the centre of the pitch!

Everything that went through him that day was world class. And he obviously did his part to contribute to the game of the century. If he didn't have a broken bone that day, then Germany could well have had another star on their badge.

The man, it would seem, was made from steel!

# SPORTSMANSHIP GONE TOO FAR?

From a man made of steel to a man made of fluffy rainbows and unicorns.

Well, that's absolutely not the way anyone would describe Italian footballer Paolo Di Canio, but there was *one* particular moment in his career that will go down in history.

It was a wintery December night in Liverpool, and West Ham were playing away at Everton. Despite it only being mid way through the season, West Ham were already desperate for points to ensure Premier League survival.

There were 5 minutes left on the clock and the game was tied at 1-1 – West Ham were on the attack. The opportunity could well have been the last chance for The Hammers to score and nick 3 points that they desperately needed.

A long ball was played into the Everton area and their goalkeeper, Paul Gerrard, was first to the ball to half clear it towards the corner flag. As he tried to run towards the ball to *ensure* it was cleared, he collapsed in agony clutching his leg. He had clearly injured himself.

The ensuing 6 seconds have gone down in history as one of the most memorable in the game.

With the keeper out of action 20 metres from his goal, the ball continued rolling towards the corner flag, where a West Ham player found it and fired a first time cross into the area.

The cross was remarkably accurate and heading towards one of the most prolific strikers in the Premier League, Paolo Di Canio.

Di Canio was great at heading, volleying and scoring outrageously good goals, so whilst the ball was in the air and heading directly at him – and given that he was unmarked – everyone in that instant *knew* that it was going to end in the back of the net.

What happened next took everyone by surprise. Di Canio grabbed the ball with his hands and immediately told everyone to stop playing so that the Everton keeper could get some medical assistance.

The Everton fans applauded him, the Everton players gave him pats on the back for the good gesture. It wasn't the same from his teammates.

West Ham captain Stuart Pearce, didn't take it as nicely. "don't let me near him, I'll kill him, I'll kill him, I'm going to rip his f*cking head off!" he was quoted as saying immediately after the game.

# THE WONDERKID THAT NEVER WAS

Every so often, you get a phenomenon in the game of football.

The likes of Pelé and Maradona come round once in a generation, and recently, we've been blessed with Ronaldo and Messi plying their trade in the *same* generation.

In between the eras of Maradona and Ronaldo/Messi, there was one kid who was blessed with more natural ability than people had ever seen.

So much so, that he was given a $1 million sponsorship agreement by Nike at 14 years of age.

He was being compared to the likes of Tiger Woods in golf and being portrayed as the football equivalent of Lebron James.

It was that same year, still only 14 years of age, that he broke into the first team of DC United and scored his first professional goal. All this a few months into becoming a teenager! He really was the real deal.

His name? Freddy Adu.

The American superstar was poised to become the greatest football player of all time. Just ask Pelé who starred in a few television commercials with the 14 year old.

His progression continued, and at 16, he was training with Manchester United, under the watchful eye of the most successful British manager of all time, Sir Alex Ferguson.

Alas, he didn't quite turn heads at Manchester United, and his career started to decline.

He had a few spells at mediocre European clubs (mostly on loan) and then went back to the USA for a while. But he never hit the heights that were expected of him.

At the time of writing, he's currently playing for a 3rd division Swedish team. A very anticlimactic ending to the most prodigious talent at the turn of the 21 century.

He claims that his failure to reach the dizzying heights he was predicted, was due to him being treated as a marketing tool from a very young age. It didn't allow him to nurture his talent and focus on his football career.

Having had an unprivileged upbringing, all the money he made as a child went towards financially helping his mum, who had worked a few jobs after emigrating from Ghana to the USA. From that perspective at least, the story does have a very happy ending.

# THE LIONESSES

It is not often that a single game of football can have a seismic cultural change on a whole country. But that's exactly what happened on July 31 2022 when England beat Germany 2-1 to win the Women's European Championship.

England had gone over 50 years without any major international triumphs in the sport. For a country that prides itself on regulating football and exporting it to the world, it was 50 years too long.

English society had grown to yearn for the football glory days - nostalgia was ingrained from a very early age in every new generation of football fan.

The whole country lived with a hopeless dream that football would one day "come home".

The thing was that '*one day*' didn't really seem like it was *ever* going to come. Until the last day of July in the summer of 2022.

The Lionesses did what no other English Team had done in 56 years. They beat Germany in a final and gave England their first senior football trophy of the 21st century.

What the lionesses did for the country, and most importantly, for millions of young fans across the country was immeasurable. They united the country at a time when it was in disarray due to a cost of living crisis and inflation. And whilst things were bad, the England team, for a short period of time, provided a bit of respite for many people across the nation.

They gave everyone in the country hope, joy and pride.

At a time when men's football still took centre stage in the country, the Lionesses victory changed that forever.

Never again would women's football be seen as anything but equal to that of their male's counterpart. A seismic change in the English societal way of thinking, and a testament to the grit, passion and determination those girls showed for their country that summer.

A real tear jerker for everyone in the country.

# CHAPTER 4
# WHEN IT'S JUST PLAIN BIZARRE

# THE STRANGEST MATCH IN MODERN HISTORY

Winning a football game is simple: Put the ball in the opposing goal more times than your rival.

The sport becomes less simple when you have a governing body come up with a rule that is *so* confusing, that it results in two competing teams trying their hardest to score own-goals!

This was the case in 1994, when Barbados and Grenada met in Concacaf's Shell Cup.

In an effort to increase the cup's popularity, the organisers required that all matches in the event had to have a winner.

In doing so they imposed a rule which stated that a Golden Goal scored in extra time would not only win a match, but also count as *two* goals.

When Barbados and Grenada met, Barbados found themselves needing to win by two clear goals to qualify for the final.

Barbados were leading 2-0 when, with 7 minutes of normal time remaining, Grenada pulled one back to make it 2-1.

A clever Barbados player informed his teammates that, given the rules of the tournament, they would be more likely to reach the final if they scored an own goal in the next 7 minutes, and then score a goal (worth two goals) in extra time.

What happened next was farcical.

The Barbadian centre back and goalkeeper played a long series of short passes between them in the 6-yard box before the defender, from 4 metres out, rocketed the ball into the back of his own net.

After the initial dumbfoundment, The Grenadians clocked on to what was going on. They also realised that they needed just one more goal *at either end of the pitch* to go through to the final (3-2 would see them win on points whilst 2-3 would see them win on goal difference).

What followed was the most unusual 3 minutes ever witnessed in international football. Barbadians were defending their own goal *as well as* that of the opposition – the Grenadians were desperately trying to score at either but had no luck.

The game went into extra time, where Barbadian ingenuity (if you can call it that) was rewarded.

They scored the Golden Goal that counted for two, and that took them through to the final of the 1994 Shell Cup.

It's safe to say that that rule was never used again in a game of football.

# A 5-MONTH-LONG GAME

On November 26 1898 referee Thomas Saywell accidentally blew for full time 10 minutes early in a match between Southampton FC and Millwall FC.

The honest mistake could not be immediately rectified by the man in black as a pitch invasion occurred.

The referee proceeded to mark the game as over with the scoreline as it was. Millwall were losing so they were incensed by the decision.

So much so that they contested the referee's decision in a tribunal, and demanded that the remaining 10 minutes be played so that they had a fair chance of winning the game.

Nothing too unusual there apart from the fact that Millwall were losing 4-1 and had very little time to draw, let alone win, the match.

That didn't stop the Londoners from kicking up a stink and fervently demanding that the game be played to its full extent.

After 5 months of deliberations, the tribunal ruled in favour of Millwall. They decided that the last 10 minutes had to be played before the end of the season.

Southampton were forced to make the 160 mile return journey to London in April 1899 to play the last 10 minutes of a game that they surely had already won. A journey that in the 19th century must have not been easy to make.

Begrudgingly they made their way to The Den to play those last 10 minutes. The result was one of the most incredible comebacks the world of football has ever seen....

...not really, those 10 minutes were the most nondescript 10 minutes of football ever seen, and the game still ended up being 4-1 to Southampton.

They went back to the south coast of England feeling like their time had been truly wasted, but at least the scoreline could be made official and Millwall could finally stop their whinging.

# WHEN THE PLAYERS COULDN'T SEE EACH OTHER

Talking about Southampton, the city is home to one of the most bizarre excuses for losing a football game.

On April 13 1996 Manchester United played Southampton at The Dell. With only a few games of the season left, they were in the thick of the title race, competing vehemently with Newcastle United to see who would take the crown of English champions.

United found themselves 3-0 down at half time – something had to be done by the manager. Traditionally it's a stern talking to to the players, but Sir Alex Ferguson had other ideas that spring afternoon.

United players went into the dressing room wearing grey and came back out wearing blue and white stripes.

Ferguson's pioneering idea for the second half was to change the colour of the kit that his players were wearing!

He hoped that this would turn the game around and see them rescue at least a draw from the game.

The team could not recover in the second half and they were beaten by Southampton in the end.

The only thing more embarrassing than the scoreline was the excuse Alex Ferguson made for the loss. He claimed that the players couldn't pick each other out on the pitch because of the colour of the kit - and that had been the reason why he'd ordered his troops to change kit at half time.

People laughed at the time, but it transpired a couple of decades later that Ferguson had been in touch with "eye scientists" at the time.

There was a growing trend in the 90s amongst elite football clubs that eye muscle training and coordination would elevate footballers to perform better on the pitch, and Ferguson quickly jumped on that trend by employing scientists from Liverpool University to help him out.

The advice from the professionals was that grey was the hardest colour the human eye could see against a backdrop of fans in a stadium. As such Ferguson kept a second kit on standby.

On that day when United had an awful first half, Ferguson thought it was down to the kit and quickly rectified it at halftime.

The world saw it as an outrageous excuse, and ultimately it did not matter. United went on to lose 3-1 and were fined £10,000 by the English Football Association for changing kits at half time.

In Ferguson's defence, you could argue that they won the second half 1-0.

# THE WORST FOOTBALL TRANSFER OF ALL TIME

Modern football now commands big money.

In looking at the worst football transfers of all time, you have to take into account the performance of the players after they signed for the new team, but also the commercial value-add to the club.

As such, the most obvious candidate for the worst football transfer of all time is Eden Hazard when he signed for Real Madrid.

He was signed as *the* marquee signing to replace one of the greatest players ever: Cristiano Ronaldo. No easy task.

Eden Hazard had indicated that he'd always wanted to play for Real Madrid. He was at the top of his game, consistently scoring goals for Chelsea. He had a year left of his contract before he could make his dream transfer to Real Madrid for free.

Real Madrid decided they couldn't wait 12 months to get him for free. Instead, they splashed out over £100 million to get him early. He rocked up to pre-season 7 kilos over-weight and scored *one* goal in the entirety of the 19/20 season.

To make matters worse, the £400,000 a week player was seen laughing with his ex-Chelsea teammates in the immediate aftermath of Chelsea knocking Real Madrid out of the Champions League. It's safe to say that Eden Hazard is not liked very much by the Real Madrid fans.

All things considered however, there is one player who takes the absolute crown for *the* worst transfer of all time, and that is Antoine Griezmann from Atletico Madrid to Barcelona.

Barcelona paid a release clause of $120 million dollars to get him to play for the club. Problem being that neither the coaches or the players really wanted him. It was a deal allegedly done by Barcelona president Josep Maria Bartomeu.

That deal put so much financial pressure on the club that they were forced to sell arguably the most talented foot-baller to ever grace this planet: Lionel Messi

Selling Messi eased some of the financial pressure. But the kicker was that, in order to get their books straight, they also had to offload Griezmann (on loan) and Suarez (for next to nothing) to Atletico Madrid - who pipped them to win the league in 2021!

Bartomeu resigned from his post after that fiasco. A disaster so big for the club, that at the time of writing, they are still recovering from it.

# THE MOST LEGEND-DAIRY FOOTBALL TRANSFER OF ALL TIME

Almost a century before that Barcelona debacle, and in an era where football was much simpler, Hugh McLenahan transferred from Stockport County to Manchester United.

McLenahan made over a hundred appearances for the Red Devils in the early twentieth century, becoming somewhat of a legend of the club and even captaining the side on a few occasions.

100+ appearances suggest that the transfer was successful on the football pitch, but what was the commercial return to the club who invested heavily in the youngster?

Well, that would depend on the value you place on ice cream.

At that time, "official" transfers didn't occur due to the game still only being an amateur sport. So United's assistant manager Luis Rocca, whose family business was in the ice cream industry, donated two freezers full of ice cream to Stockport County's fund-raising bazaar in exchange for McLenahan's services.

The player went on to score 12 goals in his United career. He really was livin' the cream before his career was cut short because of the outbreak of WWII in Europe.

# BROTHERLY RIVALRY

On June 23 2010 Ghana and Germany met in a World Cup match that made history for a very peculiar reason.

Brothers had often graced World Cup games and produced some real feel good family tales (from The Charlton Brothers for England, The De Boers for The Netherlands through to the Laudrups for Denmark), but when Jerome and Kevin-Prince Boateng met in Johannesburg in 2010, they made headlines for very different reasons. They were lining up for different teams!

Their father, Prince, moved to Germany from Ghana in 1981. A few years later he fathered Kevin-Prince with his first wife. After that marriage failed, he fathered Jerome with his second wife.

Both children would go on to represent Germany in football at youth level before Kevin-Prince switched allegiance and chose to represent Ghana. He had been unhappy about being left out of a U21 Germany squad and took the rash decision to change sides.

The two talented football players continued to rise through the ranks and play at the peak of the sport – and consequently they were selected by their nations to represent them.

When the draw for the World Cup in South Africa took place, all eyes turned to the Ghana VS Germany game as it would see brothers play against each other for the first time ever in a World Cup.

The game ended in a 1-0 victory to Germany courtesy of a Mesut Ozil goal.

Curiously enough, the brothers would go on to line up against each other again at the following World Cup in Brazil.

Interestingly, it is alleged by people close to the brothers, that George Boateng, the pair's older brother, was a much better football player than both Kevin-Prince and Jerome. Unfortunately for George, a troubled upbringing derailed his career.

# THE ANGEL WITH
# BENT LEGS

"He could do things with the ball that no other player could", said Pelé of his Brazilian teammate.

The story of one of the world's greatest ever football players begins from the day that he was born, as he was already defying the odds.

He was born with his right leg shorter than the other. His spine had curvature problems, and he was so small and fragile looking, that his family nicknamed "Little Wren". A wren is a tiny brown bird that weighs about 7 grams. In Portuguese, little wren is "Garrincha".

As an adult, Garrincha's right leg ended up being 6cm shorter than his left. He had already defied the odds to live a healthy life, let alone become a professional footballer.

Garrincha went on to become one of the most feared footballing predators of his time, leading Brazil to the 1958 and 1962 World Cup titles and being named player of the tournament AND top scorer in the 1962 finals.

Garrincha had it all. The Chilean press at the 1962 world cup were convinced he was from another planet.

He married Nair Marques in 1952 and had eight children with her. In that time, he had numerous affairs which resulted in at least 14 children with five other women. He then left his wife for a famous samba singer Elza Soares.

It is also a well known fact that Garrincha lost his virginity at 12 years old. If you find the young age somewhat surprising, then you'll be more shocked to find out that he lost his virginity to a goat.

Garrincha was not only troubled by his love of women, he also loved to drink alcohol. That would ultimately cost him his life. The little wren flew all the way to heaven in 1983, at the very young age of 49. He died of cirrhosis of the liver.

'Here rests in peace the one who was the Joy of the People' reads his tombstone.

# "I CAN GIVE YOU A HAND" - LITERALLY

In 1906 in Argentina, Barracas FC lost their goalkeeper to bitter rivals Alumni FC.

With an imminent game against Estudiantes, Barracas were scrambling to find a goalkeeper. As is often the case, one of their defenders stepped up and offered his services in between the sticks.

"I can give you a hand", Winston Coe said. "You know I can't give you two", he said in jest as he only had one arm.

With the game only round the corner, Barracas FC found themselves in a bit of a pickle. They decided to take him up on his offer, and thus giving football historians around the world a beautiful tale to tell for years to come.

Coe went in between the sticks for the game against Estudiantes, and both fans and players alike were mesmerised by Coe's performance on the day.

The Argentinean press lauded him for his confidence and shot stopping ability (apparently he saved quite a few shots that day).

Estudiantes beat Barracas 2-1 despite Coe's heroic efforts, but his performance was so good that Barracas kept him in goal for their next two games.

Unfortunately for Barracas, they went on to lose 11-0 against Reformer and 5-0 against an Alumni side that had their former goalkeeper in the team. Imagine how he felt when he walked out onto the pitch and realised he'd been replaced with a man with one arm?!

Despite the two hammerings, the Argentine press concluded that the results would have been "catastrophic" had Coe not been in goal.

With three games under his belt, Winston Coe not only taught the world a lesson in determination, he also gifted us one of the most feel-good football stories out there!

# ROHYPNOL ON THE PITCH

You would think that 'drink spiking' wouldn't happen on a football pitch, let alone in the round of 16 of a World Cup match between Brazil and Argentina.

But when two stalwarts of the game are competing for the biggest prize in world football, people will go to any length to get an advantage. Even if it verges on illegal and immoral.

It was a hot summer day in 1990 in Turin when Brazil lost to Argentina in the World Cup. Brazilian midfielder Branco said after the game that he had felt sleepy, nauseous and as if he'd been drugged. Nothing much was made of this comment, as it was perhaps a reference to the hot conditions that day.

His words took on a new meaning 15 years later, when the story re-surfaced from the mouths of Argentinean players Jose Horacio Basualdo and Diego Armando Maradona.

During the game in Italia 1990, when there was a break in play because of injury, the Argentine physio came onto the pitch carrying a cooler with some water bottles. Some were green and others transparent. Players from both sides went to drink some water from this cooler.

As Julio Olarticoechea from Argentina went to drink from one of the green containers, he got told off by Maradona: "Not from that one! From the other one…".

Meanwhile as Brazilian Valdo was drinking from the green water bottle Maradona said nothing. He was quoted 15 years later as saying that deep inside he was thinking "yeah, that's right, drink it all Valdo." Apparently Branco would then go on to finish the contents of the green water bottle - it was a stifling 40 degrees that day after all!

Finishing off that water bottle would play perfectly into the hands of the Argentines.

Branco was Brazil's set piece specialist and midfield maestro, and that day, he most certainly did have one of his quietest games ever.

The water content of those bottles was never analysed, but Maradona would go on to say on record in 2005 that the water bottle had been spiked with Rohypnol.

Apparently, as both teams were sitting on their respective coaches on the way back from the stadium, Maradona caught sight of Branco, who was pointing at him as if to say, "I know *exactly* what you did".

# LASAGNE-GATE

From one suspected case of poisoning to another.

Bitter North London rivals Arsenal and Tottenham went into the final day of the 2005/2006 season with just a point separating them.

Traditionally, Arsenal had been the more successful club and consistently had bragging rights over their rivals, but on that last day of the season it seemed as if the tide was changing.

If Spurs won their last game, they would secure Champions League qualification at the expense of Arsenal. A feat that would inject hundreds of millions of pounds into the club, elevate them to the elite of world football, and - most importantly for the fans - give them bragging rights over their arch-rivals.

Tottenham Hotspur had drawn away at Arsenal a few days earlier, and sat a point ahead of them going into their last game of the season against West Ham. However, disaster struck from an unexpected source. Or should that be sauce?

On the day of the game, all but a handful of Spurs players woke up with a crippling stomach bug. The first team was decimated and manager Martin Jol had to completely change his team around from his initial starting line up.

Spurs players had been up all night being violently sick, some continued to vomit in the dressing room before kick off. They took to the field literally running on empty, and ended up losing 2-1 to West Ham.

Arsenal won their game and leapfrogged Spurs to clinch Champions League qualification.

Conspiracy theorists immediately claimed that the Head Chef at the hotel in which Tottenham stayed that night was an Arsenal fan who had deliberately poisoned the lasagne the players had for dinner.

That theory quickly propagated on the final day of the season before an investigation took place in the hotel which dismissed the rumours.

It turned out to be a case of extreme misfortune that so many Spurs players got a stomach bug on the eve of such an important game.

# PIZZA-GATE

Incredibly, that was the second time in as many years that Arsenal were involved in an Italian food scandal.

At the time, Arsenal and Manchester United were embroiled in the biggest rivalry in English football. Together they had won the last 9 premier league titles – each meeting between the clubs became more and more hostile.

This culminated in October 2004 when Arsenal visited United on a run of being unbeaten for 49 games. They had fired up the United players by gloating about the fact that the 50th game would be achieved at Old Trafford. United didn't need any extra firing up.

The game was tense and physical. Ruud Van Nistelrooy was lucky to be on the pitch after a horrific challenge on Ashley Cole. He escaped a booking but was later fined for going in feet-first on Cole's knee and scraping his shin bone with his studs. He could have easily broken his leg.

Wayne Rooney then won a penalty for United for a minimal contact challenge and Van Nistelrooy (who should have been sent off) scored the penalty. Arsenal went on to lose their unbeaten streak and all hell broke loose after full time in the tunnel on the way back to the changing rooms.

Understandably, both sets of players were calling each other cheats in the middle of the melee. A lot of shoving was going on, and Arsene Wenger picked on Van Nistelrooy as the biggest cheat in the United team.

A full fracas broke out, things were surely going to get considerably out of hand when a pizza was lobbed across the tunnel, landing flat on Alex Ferguson's face. It dribbled down his cheek and onto his elegant suit. Time stood still.

Shoving people around was somewhat acceptable. Covering the most successful British manager in marinara sauce was a step too far. Ferguson retired to the changing room and the fight fizzled out.

For years after the event, the British press tried to discover who the culprit of this despicable act had been. The investigation (creatively dubbed 'pizza-gate'), led nowhere.

It wasn't until a few years, in a radio phone interview, that Martin Keown revealed that the person who threw the pizza had been none other than Cesc Fabregas.

# RED CARDED FOR BEING HELPFUL

When Andrew Symonds bodychecked a streaker during a cricket match in Australia in 2008, the crowd cheered, the ground security hoovered up the bruised and dazed perpetrator, and the game continued, much to everyone's satisfaction.

"I took the law into my own hands for a brief moment there and he failed to keep moving", Symonds explained.

That same year, when Argentinian footballer Adrian Bastia did *exactly* the same thing whilst playing in the Greek top flight, there was a *completely* different outcome.

It had been an uninspiring match between Panathinaikos and Asteras Tripolis, and the match was just about to finish in an uninspiring one-all draw.

During a late substitution however, excitement was injected to proceedings when a young pitch invader sneaked on.

Unlike pitch invaders in cricket, who traditionally run completely nude, this lad had all his clothes on. He was even sober enough to lead the security officials in a decent chase.

Adrian Bastia, not wanting to waste anyone's time, efficiently tripped up the streaker in passing, so security could catch him more easily.

Everyone who witnessed this action thought he had shown great initiative. Everyone except the referee who inexplicably showed Bastia a red card!

He later explained that the trip was "violent behaviour" and as such had to be punished. This was much to the bemusement of all the players and fans in the ground.

There were prolonged protests on the field from both teams. Especially because, at best, it was a yellow card offence.

The referee had his own interpretation of the law, though, and Bastia had to leave the field.

The Argentinian striker ended up leaving the field with his shoulders slumped but to a standing ovation.

# THE STRIKER AND THE
# STOLEN NECKLACE

It was 1970 and the World Cup winning captain was getting ready to defend his crown.

Bobby Moore was a towering, big-boned centre-back, a detail that will become relevant as we proceed.

On that fateful day of May 20 1970, the England team was on a tour of Colombia, playing friendlies in the Americas in the lead-up to the World Cup in Mexico.

At their hotel in Bogota, The England team was killing time in the lobby of the upmarket Hotel Tequendama. At one end of the lobby was the pricey emerald-specialist jeweller, Fuego Verde.

The players were milling around in their tracksuits, waiting for their rooms to be made ready.

Suddenly, a clamour in Spanish broke out at the doorway of the jeweller. The English players were stumped. All they could make out was that something was missing.

A young assistant pointed to a very expensive looking bracelet on the floor under the chair where England's captain was sitting. Police arrived. Bobby Moore was arrested on suspicion of theft.

This nearly caused an international melt-down. Harold Wilson, the British Prime Minister at the time, was indignant. The Colombian President was livid. He didn't want attention drawn to his home country as he battled anti-corruption allegations.

Not surprisingly, the English team quickly left Colombia to train in other countries. They left Bobby Moore behind with a team of lawyers and translators. Colombian officials wouldn't let Moore leave the country and they called him back for questioning three times!

The police had a strong case. The shop assistant swore she had witnessed Moore put his hand into an opening in the showcase and surreptitiously slip the gorgeous bracelet into his tracksuit pocket. She was very clear about this. The weakness of the case was that the bracelet in question was nowhere to be found.

In the end, Moore's lawyers were all over the testimony. Two major flaws emerged. Firstly, it was proved by demonstration that Moore's beefy hands could never have got in through the available gap in the glass case.

Secondly, the England tracksuits had no pockets!

The authorities had to let him go, and he left Colombia, never to return.

Unfortunately for English fans, The England legal team had a much stronger performance that World Cup summer than their footballing counterparts.

As for the real thief? All signs pointed to the ploy being part of the Colombian emerald cartel. It seems as if the shop assistant was part of an extortion scam that was targeting the most high-profile footballer of the time.

# FREE OR DUTY FREE? ALBANIAN TEAM IN HOT WATER

In May of 1990, the Albanian National football team had a short layover in Heathrow en route to Iceland.

They discovered that the English were a fantastically welcoming and hospitable nation. The concourse was full of shops, and all the many luxuries , almost unbelievably, were free!

They tucked in with grateful gusto. Wines and whiskeys, handbags and dresses and many wonderful souvenirs for nephews and nieces back home.

They had just been dumped from the European 1990 quali-fiers by the English, so this bounty came as something of a solace to bruised egos. Sadly, more bruising was in store for them.

As they strolled off to their boarding gate with £2,500 worth of treats stuffed in their pockets and draped around their necks, alarms were triggered from all round the airport.

The bemused Albanians were taken to the nearest station to answer for their actions.

It soon became clear that it was all big misunderstanding, and we can only imagine that the conversation in broken English must have gone something like this:

"Why did you steal all this merchandise?"

"It's free!"

"It's '*duty free*' not 'free'!"

"What does duty mean?"

After explaining that the goods weren't actually free, the authorities asked them to leave the goods behind and escorted the team carefully past any shops in time to make their flight to Reykjavik.

We have gone wild with creative freedom in recreating the conversation with authorities, but you get the gist: The Albanian players thought "Duty Free" shops meant that the goods were actually free!

# LUIS SUÁREZ'S THIRD BITE OF THE CHERRY

One of the least common offences seen on a football pitch is players biting opponents. So when broadcast cameras capture three, and *all of them* are committed by the same player, you've got to question whether there's an eating disorder at stake.

Luis Suárez's first offence came in 2010 when he was playing for Ajax against PSV. There was a strong challenge in the middle of the pitch, as is often the case in fiery derbies, and a small scuffle broke out.

It was during this scuffle that Suarez inexplicably bit Otman Bakkal in the clavicle. The referee missed it so Suarez went unpunished on the day.

However, the beauty of modern football is that there are *hundreds* of cameras filming the action, and it was one of those cameras that captured the bite. After reviewing the footage the Dutch FA gave Suarez a 7 game suspension.

A mere three years later, whilst playing for Liverpool FC, his appetite for biting re-surfaced.

In a coming together with Chelsea defender Branislav Ivanovic, the defender was left rubbing his right arm in agony. Television replays showed that Suarez had taken a bite off of the defender's arm.

The offence was again missed by the referee but he retro-spectively got punished by the Football Association of England.

Remarkably, this wasn't to be the last time he'd bite an opponent.

The next year he chomped on Giorgio Chiellini's shoulder during a World Cup game between Uruguay and Italy.

The referee *again* missed the action (he bites quickly!) but the cameras did pick it up.

Suárez claimed he was not responsible for the bite on Chiellini. Apparently he lost his balance and fell, teeth first, into Chiellini's shoulder.

A laughable excuse that makes you wonder whether he'd been successful as a child with the old "the dog ate my homework" excuse.

After that third offence the Uruguayan was banned from all football-related activities for 4 months. That must have been hard to swallow.

# YELLOW CARD, RED CARD, HAND GUN

Referees probably have the hardest and most ungrateful job in football.

It is not very often that they are praised, and the more inconspicuous they are in a game, the better they have performed at their job.

The award for the least conspicuous referee performance *ever*, must go to Gabriel Murta of Brazil.

In 2015, in an amateur match between Brumadinho and Amantes da Bola, local policeman/referee Murta was officiating the game.

Football fields, globally, are notorious for emotional outbreaks, and when Murta blew his whistle to send off an Amantes da Bola player, emotions simply overcame the player.

Swearing and gesticulating at the referee then turned into kicks and punches. That's when the ref took matters into his own hands.

He whipped out his 9mm and the world took a breathless pause. Murta's finger was on the trigger! The abusive player cooled down instantly.

Fortunately, a linesman was able to intervene and talk Murta down. He got led off gently and kindly taken away to see the local psychiatrist.

He subsequently lost his refereeing licence at a disciplinary hearing. (He was told about it in a very nice, calm way)

As for the player involved, his red card stuck. And he has been very, very respectful to referees ever since.

# THE GAME OF THREE HALVES

In the opening game of the English 1894/95 football season, referee Thomas Kirkham, was late for kick-off.

No matter. Everyone trusted a Mr. John Conqueror to take his place until the referee arrived. Hard not to trust him with a surname like that.

Conqueror was happy to volunteer his services, and the game between Derby County and Sunderland began.

Derby County were immediately on the back foot. They conceded 3 goals in the first 45 minutes.

Conqueror blew for half-time and handed the whistle over to a tardy Kirkham, who you would have thought would want to make himself inconspicuous.

Like a certain Brazilian referee a century later, he did anything but.

It was at this point that this game would go down as one of the most incredible games in the history of the sport.

Kirkham asked the Derby team if they would not prefer to start the game from scratch? Trailing by a somewhat unsurmountable 3 goals, their answer was obvious.

The little boy tasked with hanging the numbers on the scoreboard had to take down the "3" under Sunderland and put up a fresh "0" under both Sunderland and Visitors.

Mr. T Kirkham started the entire 90 minutes over again!

Sunderland kept to their original game plan. So much so that by the end of the "second half", the little boy had hung up 3-0 to Sunderland once again.

The players went into the dressing room for their second half time break and came out to plough their way through a "third half".

Sunderland, fired by a sense of injustice perhaps, were ruthless. That little boy ended up hanging five more goals for Sunderland, with a 8-0 victory for the Black Cats.

# PICKLES THE DOG AND THE MISSING WORLD CUP

England hosted and won the World Cup in the summer of 1966. They were also lucky to have a trophy to lift at the end of the event.

On the 20th of March, a mere few weeks before the beginning of the tournament, the Jules Rimet trophy disappeared from Westminster's Central Hall, where it had been on display to drum up support for the summer event.

The following day, the police received a ransom note demanding £15,000 in £1 and £5 notes if they wanted the trophy back, otherwise, the thieves claimed, they would melt the trophy down for the value of the gold.

As the police prepared a hefty operation to get the trophy back (it included printing fake notes), an unlikely new hero emerged: Pickles the black and white collie.

As pickles went for his Sunday walkies in Beulah Park, South East London on the 27th of March 1966 he stopped to sniff a package wrapped in newspaper. It was lying next to the front wheel of a parked car.

His owner, upon unwrapping it, must have been gobsmacked to discover it was the missing World Cup!

His owner received the equivalent of £100,000 in today's money as a reward for finding the trophy, but it was arguably Pickles who gained more value from the find.

Not only did Pickles get awarded the silver medal of the National Canine Defence League, but he got invited to England's celebration banquet after the team won the World Cup.

He also starred in film and television shows for the remainder of the year and won multiple "Dog of the Year" awards.

Curiously, this was not to be the first time the Jules Rimet trophy would go missing.

In 1970, the trophy was given in perpetuity to Brazil for the incredible feat of winning the World Cup three times.

The trophy sat in the Brazilian Football Federation's trophy cabinet for 13 years before it was stolen, never to be seen again.

Sadly, Pickles couldn't be called on to help find it the second time it went missing. The hero dog died in 1967 whilst chasing a cat.

His legacy will live forever as the dog who rescued the World Cup.

# THE GOAL THAT WAS "LIKE A UFO LANDING"

Disallowed goals are part and parcel of football: The ball crosses the line, the player celebrates wildly, the referee chalks off the goal, the player bashfully retracts back to his own half.

But 'allowed' goals, when the ball hasn't even been *near* the goal line, is something that doesn't happen very often in professional football.

And that's exactly what happened when Reading FC visited Watford FC on a sunny Saturday afternoon in September 2008.

In the 15th minute of the game at Vicarage Road, Reading fired in a corner and Watford defender John Eustace managed to touch the ball towards the byline - it looked as if it was going out for another corner…

However, Reading's Noel Hunt reacted very quickly, and hooked the ball back into play.

A bit of a melee ensued before the ball was kicked out of play. A goal kick was about to be given before the assistant referee spotted something that nobody else did.

The assistant referee informed the referee that when Noel Hunt hooked the ball back into play, the ball had actually crossed the goal line.

The only problem was that Hunt had actually been 3 yards away from the goal line and actually hooked it back from the byline.

The referee, to the astonishment of everyone in the ground (Reading players included!), gave the goal! Watford were livid and the Referee red carded Aidy Boothroyd, the Watford manager, for dissent.

Watford managed to claw back the deficit to 2-1, but unfortunately a late penalty to Reading meant the match ended 2-2 (despite the ball only crossing the line 3 times).

A disgruntled Aidy Boothroyd, when questioned about the goal at the post match press conference, said: "I could not believe it. It was like a UFO had just landed"

# A VERY PUBLIC WORLD CUP POO

Gary Lineker is the English darling of football.

The ex-England-striker-turned-pundit is the highest paid employee of the BBC, earning over £1m a year.

He presumably commands such a high salary due to an endearing charisma that keeps viewers glued to their television sets.

A charisma so powerful that he can get away with pooing in front of 35,000 people, wiping his bottom and hands on the grass, and still going on to earn the love and admiration of his fellow countrymen and women.

It was 1990 and England were playing Ireland in a World Cup group game in Cagliari.

Lineker had a brilliant start, scoring a goal in under ten minutes.

However, unbeknownst to his adoring fans, he was playing with an upset tummy.

In the second half a ball was hoofed up the field by Chris Waddle, and Lineker stretched as much as he could to try and reach it.

He collapsed on the floor under a challenge from an Irish defender, and whilst sitting up on the ground, did a weird sort of 'break dance' on his bum. He then ran to the opposition's area and wiped his hands on the grass.

This was all before continuing through to the semi-finals of the World Cup where England lost to Germany - Lineker establishing himself as a world class striker en route to the semi-final.

It wasn't until two decades later, that the seemingly innocuous 'break dance on his bum' that was caught by TV cameras, took on a new meaning.

Lineker confessed to the world that he couldn't control his diarrhoea that day in 1990, and he accidentally pooed himself whilst stretching for Waddle's ball.

The quick thinking attacker quickly slid on his bum to clear the mess, and did the same with his hands as he ran to receive the ensuing free kick.

It's no wonder that defenders couldn't get anywhere near him that tournament. The smell probably put them off!

# BIG SHOES TO FILL

For a country of over 1 billion people, it's surprising that India has never qualified for a World cup.

The closest they have come to playing in the prestigious event was in 1950, when – as Asian representatives – they were invited to participate by the host nation Brazil.

Their newly formed football team (India had only recently gained independence from the British) had participated in just one international event: The 1948 Olympics in London.

During that event, the Indian team featured heavily in newspapers. Not because of their stoic performances (they only *just* lost to world heavyweights France 2-1), but because their players played the game barefoot, which was unheard of in the sport.

A lot was made of this by the global press, and the world governing body had to get involved to inform India that they needed footwear in order to compete at the 1950 World Cup.

India never made it to the World Cup - it was rumoured that they had been banned from the World Cup for refusing to wear footwear to play football.

That narrative arguably fed into racist perceptions of India, and kept newspapers selling plenty of copies in the 1950s. The rumour spread like wildfire and became somewhat of an urban myth amongst football fans.

The reality was that, at a time when the sport had no commercial value, India couldn't afford to send a team to a competition that had not yet established itself as a major tournament. A lot of teams that year refused invitations to go and play in Brazil because they couldn't afford to travel such vast distances.

And whilst it is accurate to say that the global body that regulates football *did* ask the Indians to wear footwear, they did not refuse, nor use it as an excuse to boycott the 1950 tournament.

Nevertheless, this incredible urban myth is a perfect shoe-in for this book.

# ALI DIA - FOOTBALL'S BIGGEST FRAUDSTER

Ali Dia could play football - *just*.

He also alleged that he had a cousin who played football for a living, George Weah.

George Weah happened to be more recognisable than his "cousin", having been officially voted the world's best player in 1995.

Seemingly a very generous family man, "George Weah" found himself ringing football clubs in England in 1996 offering his cousin Ali's services.

He rang Rotherham and Gillingham saying that his cousin (who he had played with at Paris St Germain and internationally for Liberia) was out of a club and he was really good. They would be silly not to snatch him up.

Those clubs presumably hung up on what they believed to be a prankster calling. A clear case of it surely being too good to be true.

Dia also rang West Ham, but their manager Harry Redknapp immediately dismissed it as a wind up.

The phone then rang at Southampton FC and manager Graeme Souness picked up.

A few minutes later and we imagine the conversation went something like this:

Souness: "... Lastly George, you *promise* he's really good?"

"George Weah": "I promise. Why would I be saying this if he wasn't?"

What followed was one of the most bizarre tales in modern football.

Grame Souness, without seeing Ali Dia ever play, and simply going off a phone conversation with someone who *claimed* was the best football player on the planet, signed the midfielder on a one-month long contract.

In November 1996, and despite trepidations from the Southampton squad, Souness named Dia as a substitute for their game against Leeds.

After 32 minutes, Matt Le Tissier picked up an injury. Ali Dia was thrown on as a like-for-like substitute.

It was the worst appearance by a professional in the history of the sport. Dia was disastrous.

"He ran around the pitch like Bambi on ice," said Le Tissier. "It was very, very embarrassing to watch. We were like: 'What's this geezer doing? He's hopeless."

The team had to watch, however, bemused and horrified as the obviously uncoordinated Dia stumbled and miskicked and, most disastrously, left the team severely handicapped.

Leeds scored. After 82 minutes Souness had had enough, and subbed him off for a real player. The damage had been done, and Leeds ended up winners at 2-0.

Questions were asked and Souness revealed all.

The press called the *actual* George Weah and it was established that Weah had never called Souness, and that he didn't have a cousin called Ali Dia.

Dia himself disappeared from footballing circles soon after that.

Everything that Souness was told by the man on the phone (presumably Dia himself!) had been a lie.

For over 25 years the ex-Southampton manager has been carrying the tag of being the footballing world's most naive person ever.

Souness has gone onto relative football obscurity whilst George Weah went on to become president of Liberia. The real George Weah, that is. Not Ali Dia.

# AUSTRIA'S VERY OWN OLIVER BEERHOFF

Top performers in the world of football often get rich rewards.

In the 1994 World Cup, Saeed Owarian of Saudi Arabia scored the goal of the tournament – a marauding 70-yard run that ended in the back of the Belgian's net, Maradona-esque in every respect.

Owarian became a national icon, and on his return to Saudi Arabia, he got presented with a brand new Rolls Royce.

It seems, however, that there is an inextricable link between football and alcohol when it comes to incentives.

Take the Cosafa Castle Cup in South Africa for example, where the winner of the tournament gets a year's supply of beer from the local mega-brewery SAB.

In 1996, footballer Michael Schjonberg helped Kaiser-slautern to promotion and was rewarded by his local brewery with free beer for the rest of his life.

Not to be outdone by their German brothers, 12 years later, and perhaps feeling a little nervous at the lack of attacking threat that Austria showed in their opening Euros match, the Ottakringer Brauerei in Vienna also offered a lifetime supply of beer to the first Austrian player to score at Euro 2008.

The second game of their Euro 2008 campaign reached the 90th minute and they still hadn't scored a goal in the tournament. It would seem that the offer would go unclaimed.

But as it turned out, a Polish defender fouled an Austrian attacker during a free kick in the 93rd minute. A penalty was awarded to Austria

Up stepped Ivica Vastic, a veteran of 38 years who, with that kick, would go on to become the oldest player to ever score at a European final.

He would also *not* receive a lifetime supply of beer from Ottakringer.

Despite scoring the goal to draw the game, Austrian Football bosses intervened before Vastic could take a single sip of Ottakringer's amber nectar.

"We don't need that kind of motivation", said Alfred Ludwig, Secretary General of the Austrian Football Association.

Speak for yourself, Alfred.

# FROM SPECTATOR TO STRIKER IN THE BLINK OF AN EYE

We all have that one gobby friend who thinks they know *everything* about football. The friend that never shuts up during a game and who always thinks they know best.

Perhaps you *are* that friend if you're reading this book.

Steve Davies is definitely one of those people. And unfortunately for West Ham manager Harry Redknapp, Davies stood right behind his dugout on July 27 1994 when West Ham were playing a friendly game away to Oxford City.

Davies, an amateur footballer and West Ham fan, was giving Redknapp (who would go on to become one of England's best ever managers) an ear-load throughout the whole game.

"Why do you keep playing Chapman?! He's a f*ckin' donkey!" was the general gist of the abuse he was giving Redknapp.

The abuse centred around Lee Chapman, a centre forward who would go on to score almost 200 first team goals in his professional career. He was most certainly *not* a donkey.

Unable to field his strongest side due to injuries, Redknapp was in a bad mood, and Davies' heckling was irritating him even more. Like a sore tooth, Steve Davies got noticed.

There were even *further* injuries to West Ham during that game, and unfortunately for Redknapp, at the stroke of half time he found himself a player down and with no available replacements.

He strode over to the loud-mouthed fan behind the dugout and said "Oi, can you play as good as you talk?"

"Well, I'm better than bloody Chapman!" - Davies replied.

"Where do you play" Harry asked.

"Up front" was Davies' reply. (He actually had never played up front)

Next thing you know, Davies was being hustled down the tunnel to the changing rooms to be kitted out in the Claret & Blue. A few minutes later he came out and played for West Ham.

Davies did have *some* natural talent (he made Ali Dia look like Pelé), it was perhaps his smoking habit that let him down amongst the professionals on the pitch.

Davies was living the dream – and it was about to get truly psychedelic…

On the 71 minute mark, Matty Holmes passed to Davies, who had a moment of sublime clarity (despite the pie, two beers and seven cigarettes he'd had in the first half) and slotted past the City keeper. The pub league player had only gone and toed the ball into the Oxford City net! GOOOOAL...!

Manager Redknapp turned his eyes to the heavens in gratitude for the miracle. West Ham United went on to win 4-0.

Unfortunately for the Hammers fan, West Ham didn't give Davies a contract. They wouldn't even let him keep the shirt he played in, as the club needed it for their upcoming game against Newcastle.

After the game, the stadium announcer went over to Redknapp to ask about the striker who had scored.

"Have you not been watching the World Cup? It's the standout Bulgarian striker Tittyshiev" - Said Redknapp

"Oh yeah - I thought it was him" was the response from the announcer.

# CHAPTER 5
## SUPERSTITIONS

# THE BALD BUDDHA

Some people avoid walking under ladders, others believe a smashed mirror signifies 7 years of bad luck.

Whatever crazy beliefs people may have, they probably don't measure up to the mad superstitions most footballers have. And it seems to be endemic in the game!

From wearing the same aftershave to games, the same socks, and rubbing certain players' bellies, we've seen it all on the football pitch.

One of the most iconic superstitions comes from the 1998 World Cup, and seemingly a very successful one as they ended up winning the whole tournament. The superstition came from the French camp and its main instigators were Laurent Blanc and Fabien Barthez.

En route to World Cup glory, Blanc started a tradition of kissing the bald goalkeeper's head. After the national anthems were sung, and before kick off, the defender would go over to his goalkeeper, firmly grab his face with two hands, pull the top of his head towards him, and give a kiss on his crown.

Quite the ridiculous theatrics. The only thing is, that the more they did it throughout the tournament, the more they won.

When they reached the final, which Blanc was suspended for, the whole of France was in a panic. How would they beat the Brazilians without that pre-match kiss?

Luckily for the whole nation, just before kick off and still in his tracksuit, Blanc came out of the dugout and kissed the goalkeeper on his head. The whole of Brazil must have known it signified the impending loom.

Brazil *did* go on to have a shocker of a game — they lost 3-0 in the final.

The most superstitious of us still know it was *all* down to that lucky Blanc kiss.

# PLAYING WITH NO DEFENDERS TO UPKEEP A SUPERSTITION

You know your superstition game is strong when you leave your team playing without two centre halves because of a silly ritual.

That's what happened to Arsenal in February 2009 when they started the second half of their Champions League Round of 16 game against Roma without their two centre backs.

Kolo Toure had a superstition that he should *always* be the last person out of the dressing room before coming onto the pitch. The thing is, that on that particular evening, his centre back partner William Gallas was receiving treatment for a knock he'd picked up during the first half of the game.

The treatment went on until *after* the referee had blown for the second half to start, so Toure, true to his superstition, wouldn't come out of the dressing room until Gallas was out.

Both players sheepishly came out onto the side of the pitch, and to make matters embarrassingly worse for Toure, he rushed onto the pitch without the referee's permission, earning him a yellow card!

He said after the game that he had learned something new that evening. Surprisingly, the lesson wasn't about committing to your teammates over personal superstition, it was about him learning that he needed the referee's permission to get back onto the pitch!

# SHINPAD SUPERSTITIONS

Shin pads are an important part of the game. First and foremost, they keep players safe - having undoubtedly prevented many broken tibias over the years.

Secondly, it would seem, many football players use them in superstitious rituals before a game.

England international footballer Kyle Walker has worn the same shin pads every match day for the last 14 years. The defender, who earns over half a million pounds every month, has not once invested in a new pair since he became a professional.

That's over 500 sweaty games that he's been wearing them for. "They will always be there. I will never change them" Walker has said. Apparently they still structurally resemble a shin pad – so they just about provide enough protection to his legs…

Another player who took superstitions to a new level was ex-England captain John Terry, who claimed to have had over 50 pre-match rituals. Much like Kyle Walker, he wore the same shin pads for over 10 years, and was distraught to have lost them at Barcelona's Camp Nou once. So much so that he nearly had a panic attack thinking that the reason why they were 11 minutes from losing their following game (a cup final against Liverpool) was *all down* to the lost shin pads. Luckily they came back to win it, and Terry claimed as his own the shin pads that he borrowed from teammate Frank Lampard that day.

Terry's other superstitions included listening to the exact same artist every day before a match day (Usher for those of you asking) and parking in *exactly* the same spot every time he drove to Stamford Bridge (his home ground). He apparently went berserk for two hours before one particular game, when someone parked in his spot.

Another curious superstition came from Manchester United defender Phil Jones who would put on his right sock on first if he was playing a home game and his left sock on first if the game was away.

One of the best superstitions in world football came from the 1963 Ballon d'Or winner and Russian goalkeeper Lev Yashin. In order to calm his nerves and warm up his muscles, he would smoke a cigarette and drink a glass of vodka before every game he played.

CHAPTER 6
**FEET FEATS**

# A TRULY GOLDEN GOAL

Tahiti's footballers are a national team with almost no full-time footballers. Most work in 9am-5pm professions, and go to football practice in the evenings.

In 2012, Tahiti had a golden season. They won the Oceania Football Confederation (a FIFA regional competition) and qualified for the 2013 Confederations Cup in Brazil!

Each team member put in for leave from their day-jobs, and the Tahitian Football authority scraped together enough money for the economy-class plane tickets to South America.

The team, which included three brothers and a cousin from a single family, were down to play in a daunting draw—African Giants Nigeria, European Behemoths Spain, and South American Juggernauts Uruguay.

The question before all the encounters was simply about how *little* they could lose by.

In the end, Tahiti let in 24 goals in three matches, 6 against Nigeria, 10 against Spain, and 8 against Uruguay.

Nevertheless, the island nation of 250,000 people played stoically against overmastering odds, gaining everyone's respect and leaving fans enamoured with their determination.

The most remarkable of their feats happened in the game against Nigeria: *They scored a goal!*

A towering header by one of the Tehau brothers sent everyone watching the tournament into delirium.

Every single neutral watched through teary eyes as the Tahitian players indulged in a moment of undiluted joy - despite being comprehensively beaten.

The Tahitians celebrated the goal by pretending to row in a canoe - presumably in homage to their nation's fishing heritage. It clearly was a goal dedicated to everyone back in their home island.

A beautiful sight to behold and probably the most cheered-on goal by fans *everywhere* across the globe (probably even Nigerians at that point - it was *that* emotional).

The team returned back home as heroes, having achieved an international competition goal!

# THE MOST DISASTROUS DEBUT!

Ask any football fan about the worst debut in world history and they'll utter two words: Jonathan Woodgate.

The English defender was touted as being the next big thing after having a breakthrough season in a Leeds United side that made the Champions League semi-finals in 2001.

He was sold to Newcastle in 2002, and after a few outings for the Magpies, Real Madrid deemed him to be *that* good that they snapped him up at the end of the 2003-2004 season.

That's despite his season being riddled with injuries. *So* badly riddled with injuries that Real Madrid would not see him play for the club 13 months after they paid £13 million for him.

A million pounds for every month he laid in the physiotherapist's massage table.

By the time the 25-year-old's debut came, it had been 17 months since he had played football. Judging by his actions on the pitch that day, it looked more like it had been 17 *years*.

It was a home match, and the stands at Santiago Bernabéu Stadium were packed with 75,000 passionate fans.

Woodgate must have been picturing a dream debut where he scored. And that's exactly what he did 25 minutes into the game.

It was a rocket of a header too, 16 yards away from goal, and one that left the goalkeeper completely stunned and rooted to the spot. Unfortunately for Woodgate, it was an own goal.

Things couldn't get any worse for Woodgate... Or could they?

Within a minute of his teammates scoring two goals to counteract the one that Woodgate had scored against them, he got himself sent off. You could be forgiven for thinking he was purposely trying to sabotage Real Madrid that day.

Already on a yellow, and with Bilbao's Etxeberria running past him on the half way line, he decided the best way to stop the attacker was to bodycheck him. A silly move that cost his second yellow and a red.

Madrid's "Galacticos" were made to sweat that day, and they once again saved Woodgate's bacon. They went on to score a third goal and Madrid won the game 3-1.

Woodgate's blushes will probably never be spared, as it's hard to imagine a worse debut for a club of that magnitude.

He never managed more than three appearances in a row for Real Madrid and went back to England, to the Mighty Middlesbrough FC, at the end of his maiden Spanish season.

# THE LISBON LIONS

Out of all the incredible feats mentioned in this chapter, there are some you know will *never* happen again.

One of them is replicating what Celtic FC did in 1967.

You see, the modern day football club is built on a few pillars that determine its success: Good management, a good academy, good coaches, etc.

Arguably one of the most important foundations however, is a good recruitment strategy. Modern clubs have to trawl *every corner* of the globe to find good talent.

In 1967, Celtic won the European Cup. No biggie, right? There haven been dozens of teams to have done that since.

However, what makes Celtic FC's achievement of 1967 so mind-blowingly good, is that all of their players that season were born within 30 miles of Celtic Park.

Bobby Lennox was the rank outlier in the Scottish team that year, coming from the distant Saltcoats (a good hour's bus-ride away), followed by Tommy Gemmel, born in 11-mile distant Motherwell.

A group of lads, all born close by, taking on and slaying European Giants, is the stuff of Hollywood films.

And that's exactly what the lads from Glasgow did in 1967. The 15 Scotsmen travelled to Lisbon to line up against the mighty Inter Milan in the final of the European Cup.

The Italian giants were looking to take home yet another European Cup (having won two in the previous three finals) and took the lead in the first half.

Celtic fought back, and scored twice to beat Inter 2-1.

"There is not a prouder man on God's Earth than me at this moment", said Jock Stein, Celtic Manager on the day.

It's a pride that has continued for over 50 years at Celtic Park, and one which, given the global scale of the modern game, will never be repeated again.

# VILLAN'S VILLAIN FOUR GOAL FEST

There are only very few things in football that are more satisfying than scoring a hat-trick. One of those things is perhaps scoring 4 goals instead of 3.

That is exactly what Chris Nicholl did for Aston Villa in 1976 when they played Leicester City at Filbert Street.

And whilst there have been many players since Nicholl who have bagged four or more goals in one game, what rocketed Nicholl into the record books is that the game he scored all four goals in ended up a 2-2 draw.

A skilled centre back, Chris Nicholl often got on the score-sheet. He is often remembered for a 25 yard screamer that he scored against Everton in the 1977 League Cup final.

However it is the performance in that game that will forever make him a household legend.

Twice he put the opposition in front, and twice he made amends by clawing back the deficit that he had single-handedly imposed on his team.

After the game, Nicholl asked the referee for the ball to commemorate the event. The referee politely declined as it was his only ball (how times have changed!)

Interestingly, it was not the first time a player had scored two goals and two own goals in a game.

Sam Wynne did exactly the same thing for Oldham Athletic against Manchester United back in 1923 - although that game ended up as a 3-2 Victory to Odlham!

It seems lightning can strike twice (or eight times) on a football pitch!

# FOOTBALL'S GREATEST FAIRYTALE

A story of fantastical forces and beings, with fighters & villains, and unlikely heroes in the making. Such are the ingredients of a fairytale.

In August 2015, bookmakers across the world thought that there was more chance of finding a mythical monster in the depths of Loch Ness, than there was of Leicester City FC winning the Premier League.

Nine months later, one of those two things became a reality. As this isn't an Evolutionary Biology book, you can guess which one of the two happened…

Leicester's journey started gripping the whole world around February 2016. It was at this point that the team's position in the league (they cemented the top position after beating title favourites Manchester City) could no longer be seen as a fluke.

The world was gripped - every neutral fan in the world wanted them to continue fighting against all odds, and stay top for a few more games.

The players, who had come from humble football origins, were not only competing in the toughest league in the world, they were *beating* the richest clubs in the world.

Week in and week out, Leicester would go on to brush aside whatever team was put in front of them, and it was clear to see that legends were being made. Future World Cup winners like Ngolo Kante were emerging, and other talents like Riyad Mahrez were lighting up the league with their skill.

Like a soap opera that grips a nation, the feel good story continued every weekend, until May 2nd 2016, when other games in the league mathematically confirmed that Leicester City would be champions of England.

Out of the 38 fixtures that season they won 23, drew 12, and lost only three! They were the giant-killers of the decade, if not the century.

People the world over were in delirium. The most epic of underdog sagas had just been completed.

To top it off, it had all been overseen by their leader Claudio Ranieri, the most charismatic old man, the kind of grandfather everyone's always wanted to have. It was impossible to dislike *anything* about this fairytale story.

It is the reason why we call this game The Beautiful Game.

# THE HAND OF GOD

Sporting lingo borrows many of its phrases from war language. Sports arenas across the world are metaphorical battle grounds for the athletes.

Football is no different in that regard, and when a match takes place in the aftermath of an *actual* war, proceedings can be very poignant.

In 1982, Argentina and The UK went to war because of a disagreement over who owned two tiny little islands full of penguins in the South Pacific.

Sadly, a lot of people died in the Falklands/Malvinas war.

Four years later, England and Argentina met in the World Cup and tensions were still running high from their armed conflict. The game was a knock-out quarter final game which stoked the proverbial embers of the war.

Two of the most remarkable things in World Cup history happened over the course of the following 90 minutes.

In the first half, a young Diego Maradona waltzed around the English back line before trying to play a one-two with his team mate. Maradona was *so* good that he got the *English defender* to play the one two for him - the defender accidentally looping the ball into the 6 yard box.

English goalkeeper Peter Shilton was just about to punch the ball away, when the little Argentinian magician* jumped up and used his hand to nudge the ball into the back of the net. An illegal move that was so audacious in nature that everyone in the ground was wondering why he was crazy enough to celebrate it like he was. The problem was that the referee didn't spot the infringement and allowed the goal to stand.

Maradona didn't wait too long to admit his guilt. After the match he said it wasn't his hand that scored the goal, but rather "the hand of God".

To make matters worse for the English, four minutes later Maradona danced his way around half a dozen English players before slotting the ball past English goalkeeper Peter Shilton. It was one of the most beautiful sights global football has ever seen. True poetry in motion. It became known as "The Goal of the Century".

The narrative of that game, which was so intrinsically linked with the recent war between the two countries, produced two of the most talked about episodes in World Cup football.

And although a football game will never surmount in importance the tragedy of human sacrifice at war, what the

Argentinian players achieved that day was seen as some-what of a collective act of redemption for what many Argentineans felt was an unjust war fought on the doorstep of their country.

*cheat (depends on your personal views)

# THE MOST DISLIKED UNDERDOG

If there was ever a national equivalent to Leicester City's triumph in 2016, then it's safe to say it was Greece in 2004.

However, the way they achieved it was more of a hardship tale than a fairytale for football fans.

Greece arrived in Portugal for the European Championships as 150-1 outsiders.

It wouldn't be too harsh to say that when they got there, they were merely making up the numbers. After all, they had *never* won a match at a major tournament before.

Greece got drawn in the Group of Death—with Spain, Russia, and Portugal—and that is where they were expected to drown.

Their chances of even making it out of the group stages were so slim that even Greek left back Takis Fyssas booked his wedding date for July 9 that year, telling his fiancé that it would give him a couple of weeks to prepare for their big day.

Little did he know, that with Otto Rehhagel at the helm, he'd have an even *bigger* day five days before his wedding.

The Greek started by beating the host nation, Portugal, in the opening game, surprisingly scoring *two* goals past them!

They then went on to draw with Spain 1-1 and lose 2-0 against Russia. Miraculously they scraped through the group.

In the quarter finals they faced recent World Cup winners France. They scored a solitary goal and then proceeded to 'park the bus' on their goal line. The tactics worked for Rehhagel and they scraped through to the semi-finals to face the Czech Republic.

After 90 minutes of semi-final action, the scores were tied at 0-0. In the 105th minute they scored a silver goal that sent them through to the final, where they were to meet Portugal again.

You can guess what happened in the final. Greece sat back and absorbed Portuguese pressure for 57 minutes. It was then that Angelos Charisteas decided to score a goal, allowing Greece to then sit back and absorb Portuguese pressure for the last 33 minutes of the game.

The minnows of European football achieved an outrageous feat by winning the European Championship that year, and Otto Rehhagel gave the world a defensive football masterclass that summer. Or, he bored everyone around the world to bits that summer - it really depends if you're a glass half full or half empty kind of person.

One thing he certainly did do, was prove that the best form of attack was a good defence - something that Jose Mourinho took to new levels the following decade.

# THE GREATEST THREE LEAF CLOVER

Liverpool have been there or thereabouts. Manchester City have missed it by a whisker. The Invincibles of 2004 didn't even get near it. It's an almost *impossible* feat to achieve.

Only one English team has ever won what most consider the most elusive of football records: Winning The Premier League, The UEFA Champions League and the Football Association Cup in one season.

In 1999, Manchester United did just that. And they did it in one of the most dramatic fashions The Champions League has ever seen

Having been crowned domestic League and Cup Champions earlier in the month, Manchester United went into the Camp Nou in Barcelona, on the 26th May 1999, knowing that a victory against Bayern Munich would seal their fate as immortals of the game.

Their route to the final hadn't been easy. Italian teams were at the pomp of their glory in the 90s, and United came across both Inter Milan and Juventus en route to the final. The former was dispatched relatively easily, the latter - at home in the first leg - saw them come from behind to snatch a draw from the jaws of defeat.

It was during the return leg in Turin that the fairy tale started to write itself.

Roy Keane, the captain of the team, picked up an early yellow card that meant he would miss the final through suspension. Cue the best performance of his career - a selfless performance that would see him score a goal, leave *everything* on the pitch and inspire his teammates to victory.

United would also lose Paul Scholes to suspension for the final. Their best two central midfielders suspended for the biggest game in the Club's history. They were up against it in Barcelona. And it showed.

For 89 minutes in the final, United players were very average. They were second best to the German giants throughout the game and rode their luck time and time again. Bayern looked to have sealed the 1-0 victory going into the final minute of the game. (they should have been 2 or 3 nil up by this stage)

United got a corner. They were desperate for something, so much so that their own keeper was in the opposition box.

Up stepped David Beckham who pinged the ball beautifully in the German box. Munich somehow scrambled it away, but only to Ryan Giggs who took a wild shot (so weak in nature) that Sheringham managed to guide it into the back of the German's net.

United managed to draw the game in the final minute and they had bought themselves some extra time to try and win the game. Incredible Scenes!

Before extra time came however, United got another corner.

Beckham did his thing again and, with literally only a dozen or so seconds left on the clock, he delivered an inch perfect cross into the German box. Munich defenders rose to get it away but Sheringham got there first. He nodded it down to Solskjaer who stuck a leg out.

The ball ricocheted off of his outstretched leg and into the roof of the net. United had won the Treble in the most dramatic of ways.

Solskjaer ran to the corner and slid on his knees in jubilation, tweaking his medial ligaments in the process. The injury would never really matter however – he had just made history.

His teammates piled on and celebrated the greatest ever comeback in Champions League history.

The world would never see such drama in a final again, until 6 years later in Istanbul when AC Milan and Liverpool met…

# LIVERPOOL'S LAST GASP GOAL GLUT

AC Milan were cruising to victory in the UEFA Champions League Final of 2005. They were 3-0 up at half time, and their opponents, Liverpool, were simply outgunned.

As the players trudged back to their dressing rooms, neutral fans couldn't help but feel a sense of embarrassment for the Liverpool players.

They had made it to the final of club football's most prestigious competition only for their pants to have been metaphorically pulled down by the opposition. AC Milan had toyed with them, ridiculing them for 45 minutes.

What AC Milan had done in the initial 45 minutes was undone in 7 second half minutes by Liverpool.

Captain Steven Gerrard (who had been anonymous in the first half), scored his first headed goal for the club in four years. What a time to break that run. He inspired Vladimir Smicer to score a second two minutes later, before being brought down in the box by Gennaro Gattuso and earning Liverpool a penalty kick.

Xabi Alonso stepped up to the plate and had his penalty kick saved before scoring from the rebound. Incredibly, AC Milan capitulated and Liverpool found themselves back in the game.

After a few near misses by AC Milan, the teams found themselves going into a penalty shootout after 120 minutes of football played. All was set for the goalkeepers to shine. The Dudek-Dida show.

Dudek most certainly stole the show. Not just because of his dancing antics on the goalline as the opposition lined up to take penalties, but because he saved a penalty from dead ball specialist Andrea Pirlo.

At 3-2 a piece in the penalty shootout, the European Footballer of the Year, Andriy Shevchenko, stepped up. His meek penalty was saved by Dudek and mayhem ensued in Istanbul. Liverpool had just won the trophy after being 3-0 down at half time.

The unlikeliest of comebacks had just taken place. Liverpool gave the world a lesson in grit, determination and perseverance that evening and sealed a much deserved victory in the Champions League.

# THE BUSBY BABES - RISING FROM THE ASHES

The beauty of football clubs is that they transcend the sport itself. They foster community in a way that very few other things do, and that's both in times of elation and tragedy.

Fewer tragedies come as sad as the one which engulfed Manchester United on February 6 1958. It is also a story of endeavour and determination that highlights the grit some people show to overcome even the most harrowing of tragedies.

In 1958, Matt Busby's Manchester United, were current English champions and competing bravely in Europe.

The team was very young, energetic and was showing flair that football at the time had seldom experienced. They were causing so much furore that they became known as The Busby Babes. They were so good that even rival fans had a soft spot for them (unheard of now for Manchester United rivals!)

The team had just qualified for the semi-finals of the European Cup, when they boarded a plane back to England from Belgrade. The plane made a stop in snowy Munich to re-fuel. As the pilot went to take off, he aborted his first attempt - conditions were dreadful.

He tried to take off for a second time, but again, that was aborted. The slush of the melting snow was slowing the plane down too much for it to achieve lift off.

It was third time unlucky for Manchester United. The plane veered off the runway in its third attempt at taking off - it simply couldn't get enough speed for take off due to the slush - and crashed through a fence into a house.

As the plane caught fire, survivors tried to rescue as many people from the wreckage as they could. Goalkeeper Harry Gregg not only saved Bobby Charlton and Dennis Viollet from the burning fuselage, but also a 20-month old baby from another fellow passenger.

In total, 23 people lost their lives in the crash. Eight of those were Manchester United players.

The Board of Manchester United voted to dissolve the club - after all, half of the first team had just lost their lives.

Manchester United would have ceased to exist there and then if it wasn't for the inspirational coach Jimmy Murphy who argued that it wasn't the United way to fold in the face of tragedy, but in fact, to do the exact opposite.

Murphy rustled together a few players on loan from around England and only three months later reached the final of the FA Cup. The team played with phoenixes on the badge that day to symbolise their rise from the ashes. Unfortunately for United, they lost the final 2-0 to Bolton.

Amongst the survivors of the crash were Bobby Charlton and manager Matt Busby. Busby was the son of a coal miner—he knew how to dig deep. A mere ten years later, and having had to start from zero after being on the cusp of European glory, he led Manchester United to the European Cup for the first time. A side that was captained by Bobby Charlton.

A truly remarkable story of a side decimated by tragedy rising from the ashes to win club football's biggest prize.

# WINNING A TOURNAMENT THEY DIDN'T QUALIFY FOR

At the end of June 1992 the Danish National side were flying back to Denmark with the Euro '92 trophy. They had not even qualified to be there!

10 days before the tournament was due to start, Yugoslavia got disqualified because of international conflict. The Danes, who had come second in Yugoslavia's qualifying group, got catapulted into a group that contained Sweden, France and England.

Denmark were so unprepared that they played their first game in the under-21 kit – as their sponsors were still scrambling to produce a rush order on senior shirts and shorts.

Everyone (Danes included) thought they were there quite literally to make the numbers.

They drew against England in the first game.

Their second game saw them lose to Sweden, after which, the commentator famously said "Denmark are out of the European championship, how awful is that?".

The commentator was simply not expecting the Danes to beat a French team led by Eric Cantona and the Swedes to beat World Cup semi-finalists England.

That's exactly what happened, but reality was *surely* about to set in. Denmark were up against The Netherlands, winners of Euro '88. A side containing an almost incredible mix of legends of the game *and* upcoming talent.

The names of Rijkaard, De Boer, Koeman, Gullit, Bergkamp and Van Basten stood between Denmark and a place in the final.

The game went to a penalty shootout after ending 2-2.

Schmeichel decided he was going to dive left for the first penalty in the shootout. Regardless of who was taking the first penalty.

He looked up and realised it was no other than Marco Van Basten standing in front of him. Choosing a side is perhaps a bit futile when one of the greatest ever strikers is standing in front of you - the likelihood is that it's going to be a goal *even if* you pick the correct side.

But a change of guard took place that very moment - Van Basten went right and Schemeichel saved. The keeper earned his promotion to legendary status straight away.

The Danes went onto the final against The Germans, where a beautiful and poignant sub-story emerged – Kim Vilfort being the tragic hero at the centre of it.

The Danish midfielder had gone back to his home country to be with his daughter who had leukaemia. But she insisted that he played in the final. He fulfilled his daughter's wishes and returned to Sweden to play the final.

In the final, Denmark were beating Germany 1-0.

12 minutes from time, Vilfort scored a goal to make it 2-0. It was game over for the Germans and minnows Denmark, who hadn't even qualified for the tournament, had just created history by winning Euro 1992.

Vilfort's daughter sadly passed away a few weeks later, but it seems she didn't want to give up her fight before seeing her daddy become a European champion.

# BRAZIL'S GREATEST EVER HUMILIATION

Brazilians, it seems, are genetically modified to be talented at football.

Generation after generation they have thrived on the international stage, being the most successful team in the history of the sport with 5 World Cups.

So when they were playing at home in the semi-final of the 2014 World Cup - it was inevitable that they'd progress to the final.

Then again, the Germans ain't bad at football either - and their history has perhaps shaped the nation to be ruthless when competing.

What Germany did to Brazil on the evening of July 8 2014 in Mineirão wasn't even ruthless - it was torture.

It was the cold blooded massacre of the joy of 200 million people. The collective happiness of a country sapped out of them in 90 fateful minutes.

Neither Germany nor Brazil had dropped a point on their way to the semi-finals. And the Brazilians were favourites to win the tournament given they were playing on home turf.

When the game kicked off, Brazil were quick off the traps and got a corner after 37 seconds. That would be as good as it got for them.

Before the half hour, Müller, Klose, Kroos (twice) and Khedira had put Germany 5-0 up.

In scoring that goal, Klose overtook Ronaldo as the leading World Cup scorer in history. Ronaldo himself was watching in the stands - talk about adding salt to the wound.

Schürrle scored another brace before full time to make it 7-0.

Poor old Oscar dos Santos Emboaba Júnior's goal in the 90th minute could not be considered a "consolation" goal. Nothing could console the Brazilians for a 7-1 drubbing by Germany. No side had ever lost *that* badly in a World Cup semi-final.

Brazilians call it the *Mineirazo*, the Agony of Mineira. Funny that they named it because nobody in Brazil ever, ever speaks of it.

# "AGÜEROOOOOOOOOOO...."

There will never be a more dramatic final day of a Premier League season than the one witnessed in 2012.

Going into the beginning of the season, Manchester City had just won their first trophy in 35 years. It seemed the "noisy neighbours" of the most successful club in English history were beginning to assert their dominance.

Especially when they beat Manchester United 6-1 at Old Trafford that season. A result so shocking that it prompted Paul Scholes to come out of retirement to help his club.

Throughout the season, the two teams battled it out in a topsy turvy clash at the top of the league – often trading places at the top of the ladder –so it was no surprise that both teams reached the final day of the season level on points.

City had a superior goal difference so it meant that going into the final day of the season they had to beat or match

United's result to be crowned champions of England for the first time in 44 years.

City were playing QPR who needed a result to avoid relegation. And they were managed by Mark Hughes who had just been sacked by City. The game obviously meant a lot to everyone, and not least to Joey Barton who got himself sent off.

Over in Sunderland, Manchester United beat the hosts - and as the game finished there were some smiles starting to emerge on the United players as they heard that City were losing 2-1 at The Etihad in the 90th minute.

There was plenty of injury time to be added on at the City game because of the Barton sending off, and it was during this added time that the miracle of Manchester happened.

In the 92nd minute, Edin Dzeko headed in David Silva's corner!

At this point, The Red Devil's win over Sunderland still trumped a Citizen's draw. The title was still United's.

But two minutes is a long time in football - and this is all it took for Aguero to play a one-two with Ballotelli on the edge of the box, drop his shoulder and take a shot at goal.

The shot rifled into Chris Kirkland's net and The Etihad went wild. The commentator of the game howled an incredulous "Agüeroooooooooooooo…." that has now gone down in history as one of the most famous lines in British broadcasting history.

Manchester United were denied a 20th English crown in the cruellest of ways, and Agüero forged his name into history books of Manchester City by almost single hand-edly earning City their first Top flight English crown in 44 years.

# THE GREATEST CUP RUN IN THE WORLD

The story of Calais Racing Union FC is *the* Cinderella equivalent of amateur football fairy tales.

"The Magic of The Cup" is a phrase dished around when semi-professional footballers come head to head with the footballing greats, and there are often giant maulings which make for feel-good stories. But if there's one way to make a feel-good story feel even better, it's when the footballers aren't part-timers, but complete amateurs.

That's exactly what happened in the 1999/2000 Coupe de France when Calais Racing Union had the best cup run *any* amateur side had ever seen.

After beating four fellow amateur sides and one semi-professional side, they came up against their first fully professional side - Lille, who were in league 2.

The game went to penalties and they got their first major scalp.

After defeating a fifth-tier side, they were drawn at home against Strasbourg of League 1.

Their 2,100-capacity stadium couldn't contain the excitement of the people of Calais, so they had to book 65 coaches to transport people to Lens's stadium - and how worth it it was, they beat Strasbourg to set up a semi-final clash with Bordeaux.

The town went wild! This was a team of electricians, social workers, and supermarket workers. Workers who made a living by packing bags full of booze for drunk English tourists!

They were about to battle it out on the pitch against the reigning champions of France. A team that contained many experienced internationals and even a recently crowned World Cup winner in Christopher Dugarry!

The rules in France state that the lower league side is always the home team in a Coupe de France game.

Bordeaux brought 40,000 fans with them to Lens, Calais' temporary home. Calais' manager, Ladislas Lozano, would have to tell his troops to brace themselves for the onslaught.

Survive the onslaught they did. After 90 minutes the game ended in a draw. The match then went to extra time where Calais won 3-1!

Absolute Pandemonium in Calais! Lozano had a minor heart attack and had to be briefly hospitalised. He even had the President of France, Jacques Chirac, ring him up in hospital to make sure he was OK. They had well and truly captured the imagination of everyone in the country.

And the players were getting financial recognition too. Prize money for the Calais side after that game was £10,000 each! A fair increase from the small change in tips that the bag packers received from boozy English tourists in supermarket car parks!

So the amateurs went onto the final at Stade De France, which had only recently been the venue for another final - *the World Cup final*.

Only Nantes stood between Calais and arguably the single greatest football story ever.

Calais took the lead in the 34th minute of the game. We were about to see the unthinkable…

Unfortunately that's where the fairy tale stopped. Nantes went on to score two goals and win the game.

At the trophy presentation, the Nantes captain invited the Calais captain to accompany him. They lifted the trophy together in one of the most beautiful scenes competitive football has ever seen.

Calais gained the hearts of the French nation that year - they were well and truly the people's champions.

# THE GREATEST STRIKING PARTNERSHIP EVER

With so many talented players in a modern football team, you often get goals from everyone on the pitch: wingers, strikers, full backs - hell, we've even mentioned a few goalkeepers already in this book who have put the ball in the back of the old onion bag.

There was a time, however, when only strikers got the bulk of the goals for a team, and with a 4-4-2 formation the norm for a long time, it was a sight to behold when your two forwards up front went together like bread and butter.

There have been some *incredible* partnerships.

Pelé and Garrincha mesmerised the world and won plenty of World Cups over the course of a couple of decades.

Andy Cole and Dwight Yorke seemed to dance around defenders with telepathic ability for Manchester United in the late nineties.

The modern great partnerships include the likes of Van Basten and Gullit for Holland, Inazghi and Del Piero for Juventus and a young Ronaldo and Rooney at Manchester United.

The most memorable of mentions must go to Luis Suarez and Lionel Messi. They teamed up at Barcelona for a mere 6 years and scored over 400 goals in that time. Let that sink in. *Four hundred*. It almost defies belief.

However, all great partnerships, much like Adam & Eve (if you're religiously inclined), have an almost miraculous-like inception. And the Bing Bang of partnerships (if you're not religiously inclined) must go to the OGs of this movement: Ferenc Puskas and Alfredo Di Stefano.

The Hungarian and Argentinean teamed up at Real Madrid in the 1950s and revolutionised the way football was being played at the time. Never had the world seen such an artistic understanding on a football pitch result in such an abundance of goals. They performed their craft with elegance and ease.

The epitome of their partnership, and something that hasn't been replicated ever since, came in the European Cup final of 1960 when Real Madrid won their 5th consecutive European Cup.

Their opponents on the night were Eintracht Frankfurt who were obliterated 7-3. Di Stefano bagged a hat-trick in that final. And the other four goals scored by Real Madrid were all scored by his partner Puskas.

It was a time when football was just starting to be shown on TV, and audiences across the world had never seen a partnership that prolific before. Over 60 years laters, and the world has never seen one since…

# THE GREATEST DEFENDING PARTNERSHIP EVER

Strikers tend to take most of the plaudits in world football. But not in this book - this chapter is for the Puskas and Di Stefanos doing it hard on the other side of the pitch.

Like some of the aforementioned partnerships, some deadly defending duos spring to mind when you think of contenders for the best *ever*.

Godin and Miranda's reliance at the back of Diego Simeone's Atletico Madrid catapulted the club from relative European minnows to European finalists.

Nemanja Vidic and Rio Ferdinand at the heart of the Manchester United defence allowed the Red Devils to win countless trophies in the early noughties.

Franco Baresi and Alessandro Costacurta single handedly allowed Italian international football dominance to flourish in the 80s (both at club and international level) - it was a metaphorical brick wall built on strong foundations.

Foundations that only kept getting stronger as their 20 year partnership progressed. The pair gobbled up nearly every trophy they competed for and showed the world that defending was a beautiful art too (If only Mourinho lived in that era!)

The renaissance for artistic defending had begun a few years earlier in Germany though. And that can be credited to Franz Beckenbauer, The Kaiser (mentioned in chapter 3), who moved from a tough tackling midfield position to grace the heart of Bayern Munich and Germany's defence for countless seasons.

He would not have been able to perform to the ability to which he did if it hadn't been for the man they called 'The Kaiser's Bodyguard': Hans-Georg Schwarzenbeck. He was happy to let his captain take the limelight, but together they won 15 major trophies, including 4 Bundesligas, 3 European Cups, and the 1974 World Cup.

Not many defensive partnerships have won more trophies than those two. And when you find one that does, it takes the prize of best defensive partnership *ever*.

Enter Gerard Pique and Carles Puyol.

Together they won *everything* there is to win in world football.

Not only that, but they did it at a time when their opposition was out of this world (almost quite literally when you consider they often kept Real Madrid's "Galacticos" at bay).

At a time when the Rooneys, Cristiano Ronaldos, Kloses, Ronaldos etc. were at their peak, Pique and Puyol not only stopped those powerhouses from playing their game, but often ridiculed their ability by not letting them have an inch of the ball.

At club level they have 7 Champions League medals between them. As well as 5 Super Cups and Club World Cup medals. Between them they also have 14 La Liga and 9 Copa del Rey medals.

At international level they both won the European Cup and the World Cup. And the way in which they did it both for Spain and Barcelona was delightful.

The pair combined grace and power beautifully, but it was their reading of the game that made them stand out. They could tackle hard when needed (matching The Netherlands in that very aggressive World Cup final in 2010), *and* also majestically come out playing with the ball at their feet when required to do so. Especially when the duo were playing under Pep Guardiola at Barcelona.

They had it all. True maestros of the art of defending.

# CHAPTER 7
## UNLUCKY, SON!

# GHANA TAKE SOME TIME TO RECOVER FROM THAT ONE!

The first ever World Cup to be hosted in Africa took place in the summer of 2010.

The Ghanaians had a golden generation of a team and they were the undoubted people's favourite as the tournament progressed.

They were poised to have a chance to battle it in the semi-finals for a place in the final, had it not been for the most dramatic act of skullduggery a World Cup has ever seen.

Ghana and Uruguay were tied at 1-1 and the game went into extra time. In the last minute of extra time, there was a mad scramble in Uruguayan's box.

In an act of defending desperation, Luis Suarez stopped the Ghanaians from scoring by punching the ball away from his goal line.

For those unfamiliar with the name, Luis Suarez was NOT the Uruguayan goalkeeper. He was Uruguay's striker, and he had just committed the most fragrant and obvious act of cheating the world had ever seen. (What would Paolo Di Canio think?!)

Ghana would have won the game had Suarez not cheated. Instead, they got compensation in the form of a penalty kick.

It was the last kick of the game and they were given the chance to win the game (again) if they scored that penalty kick.

Up stepped Asamoah Gyan who rocketed his shot against the crossbar. Suarez, who was watching from the tunnel (he had been sent off for cheating) celebrated as if he'd just won the World Cup.

It was the most unjust and dramatic quarter final the world had ever seen. The people's champions had been swindled out of a semi-final spot in the first world cup held in their continent.

Ghana went on to lose the game on penalties. Gyan, understandably, was inconsolable after the game. The Uruguayans celebrated wildly into the night.

The Uruguayan manager was not happy Suarez was being labelled a cheat: "Calling it cheating is too hard. It could have been a mistake", he said.

A mistake it was most definitely not. Ask any Uruguayan to this day, and they will tell you it was the greatest act of self-sacrifice the footballing world has ever seen.

# SEEING BLACK... THEN RED!

Some sendings off you cannot argue against. Think about Zidane's headbutt mentioned in chapter one. Clear as day.

Others are very subjective and the referee's decision is driven by fans' passion, or by skewed interpretation of the laws of the game.

But there is a player in Argentina who could well be right in thinking he's the most hard-done-by recipient of a red card in the history of the game.

Juan Pablo Krilanovich was playing a game for Lanus Reserves as a midfielder. The tactics were simple from the coach: Apply pressure *everywhere* on the pitch. Something straight out of the Jurgen Klopp book of coaching.

So when the midfielder was high up the field, applying pressure on the back line of Banfield Reserves, Banfield central defender Lautaro Cardozo panicked.

The age old mantra of "when in doubt kick it out", came straight to him, and that's exactly what he did - booted the ball as hard as he could.

Unfortunately for Kirlanovich, he was doing his job of pressing so well (and so quickly!), that his face was right in the way of the defender's clearance.

The ball hit the midfielder's face, making him lose consciousness. As a result, his legs stopped functioning properly, and with momentum still in full force, he stumbled towards his opponent.

He landed awkwardly on the opposition's leg and twisted the defender's knee. Two players out for the count.

One with a suspected twisted knee, and the other with a concussion.

Kirlanovich's concussion didn't last long - he woke up a couple of minutes later and was given a straight red by the referee for his clumsy challenge on Cardozo, which unfortunately, did break the defender's leg.

To the best of our knowledge, it's the first red card for an unconscious incident on a football pitch.

You can just about hear Kirlanovich's pleading: "But Ref, I was *UNCONSCIOUS*!"

# THE CHAMPIONS LEAGUE THAT 'SLIPPED' AWAY

Ask any football fan, and they will tell you that when a game goes to penalties, it's a lottery as to who will win.

One of the unluckiest moments on a football pitch happened on a wet Moscow evening in 2008.

Manchester United and Chelsea had gone head to head in the Premier League that season, with United *just* coming out on top after the last game of the season.

So when the teams met in the final of the Champions League, it couldn't have been a closer affair.

The game ended 1-1 and went to penalties. Didier Drogba had been sent off in extra time so he wouldn't have the opportunity to take a penalty.

A very unusual occurrence happened during the shootout: Cristiano Ronaldo *missed* his penalty.

And he missed that penalty in the last game of a season where he had scored 42 goals (including one in *that* very final).

It was extremely surprising and unusual. But such is life. The world's best player had, somewhat ironically, cost Manchester United the chance to win the world's biggest club trophy. Or so it seemed...

John Terry stood 12 yards from goal ready to kick into a net only guarded by Edwin Van Der Sar. Score the penalty and Chelsea win the Champions League. Easy as that.

As John Terry took his kick (Van Der Sar diving the opposite way to the ball), he slipped on the wet Moscow grass and his shot hit the post.

Manchester United not only got back into the shootout but ended up winning it lifting the Champions League trophy.

John Terry cut a desolate figure as he left the pitch in tears.

Had Dider Drogba been on the pitch, he probably would have taken the deciding penalty (like he did in Munich 4 years later) and won the game for Chelsea.

The unluckiest slip of all time, bar maybe Steven Gerrard's in 2014, but this one was somewhat more conclusive of failure.

# THE BALL IS IN ORBIT

There's perhaps only one penalty that is more infamous than John Terry's.

And that is because the only thing worse than your penalty miss denying your team immediate victory, is your penalty miss *gifting* the opposition immediate victory.

Imagine that happening in the only game that is more important than a Champions League final, the World Cup final.

Roberto Baggio does not need to imagine that scenario — he was at the epicentre of it in Los Angeles, California in 1994.

Roberto Baggio was Italy's talisman, having been one of the world's best players for a couple of years leading up to the tournament.

So when he was given the responsibility of keeping Italy in the game by taking the fifth penalty, no one doubted his ability to score. He had, after all, been carrying the team through the whole tournament.

There he was, mano-a-mano with Brazilian goalkeeper Claudio Taffarel, when he took his penalty. He had to score to keep Italy in the game. A miss would mean the Italians lost the World Cup.

Baggio took the shot. The ball scooped over the bar - very high over the bar - and the Brazilian players invaded the pitch in joy at just having won the World Cup.

That was *the* miss that gifted the opposition the biggest trophy in world Football. It's hard to know whether Baggio has ever recovered from that incident.

Scientists are currently undecided as to whether Baggio's shot will crash on land *or* water upon re-entry from orbit.

# THE WORLD'S WORST TACKLE

Whilst Baggio's shot left the stadium *over* the stands, some World Cup moments are remembered by players sadly leaving via ambulances.

This was the case of Patrick Battiston, who was unfortunately left in a near state of a coma, when he was the victim of the World Cup's most vicious foul ever.

In the 1982 World Cup, France and Germany came head to head. At one point during the game, Michele Platini played a delightful through ball to his French striker, Battiston. Battiston ran towards goal to make a connection with the ball. The opposing German goalkeeper, Harold Schumacher was also running towards the ball.

Battiston made contact with the ball before Harold Schumacher, who, in a callous disguise at attempting to clear the ball, simply kept charging towards Battiston. He let his momentum carry him forward, and in the middle of the air, twisted his hip to make contact with the body of the frenchman.

Battiston slumped onto the floor, his limbs collapsing next to him. The scenes were reminiscent of a highway accident. Extraordinarily, it took 7 minutes for the stretcher to arrive to take him to the ambulance. Platini later recalled how Battiston's limp body was cold and pulse-less. He feared for his teammate's life.

The French striker lost three teeth, damaged his spine and broke two ribs in the collision with Schumacher.

In the post match interview, Schumacher (who should have been sent off but made a telling contribution to the game) said he would pay for the Frenchman's new set of teeth, apparently showing little regard for the seriousness of the injury and leading to tense Franco-German relations.

To add salt to the wound, the referee never gave a foul for the incident. He awarded a goal kick to the German goalkeeper.

# MISSING MORE BEAUTIFULLY THAN OTHERS SCORE

When a nice move on the pitch doesn't result in a goal, it is often quickly forgotten. But not in the case of The King, Edson Arantes Do Nascimento Pelé, who 'scored' the greatest goal that never was.

When he missed the goal, the world took notice. The things he did with his body in the lead up to that miss had never been seen before in the world of football.

Football changed that day from being more than just a sport, it became an art. People realised that there was something more beautiful to the beautiful game than just scoring.

So how *exactly* did the most beautiful miss ever unfold? It happened in the 1970 World Cup when Brazil were playing Uruguay.

Tostao stole the ball from a Uruguayan player and played a delightful, perfectly weighted through ball to Pelé.

Pelé accelerated towards the ball at the same time as the Uruguayan keeper was. It seemed as if they were both going to get to the ball at exactly the same time.

It seemed inevitable that they were both going to collide on the edge of the box. As a matter of fact, what was unfolding was almost a carbon copy of the situation that happened twelve years later with Schumacher and Battiston. But Pelé was ahead of his time.

In a second that seemed a lifetime, Pelé did nothing but let the ball run past him. But no one does 'nothing' more elegantly than The King. For that split second he danced, played and mesmerised. Danced with the ball, toyed with the keeper, and mesmerised millions.

Pelé's clever manoeuvre led to the keeper finding himself 25 yards out of his goal, with ZERO clue as to where the ball was. Talk about looking silly.

Pelé knew exactly what he was doing, and without even touching the ball, found himself with an open goal (albeit a VERY tight angle).

He took his shot, and incredibly, missed. The ball trickled a few yards wide from the post.

The game changed that day, however. The greatest miss of all time showed us all that football was not a game of brute force, but indeed was the beautiful game.

# CHAPTER 8
## IT'S ALL POLITICS

# THE MOST POLITICALLY CHARGED GAME EVER

Football is the sport of the masses, and politicians will always want the support of the masses.

Therefore, it's somewhat inevitable that football and politics will forever intertwine.

Iran and USA were drawn together in a group stage game of the World Cup in France in 1998. This had ripple effects across the whole globe as the relationship between the countries was very hostile. It had been very hostile for the two decades prior to that, since the Iraninan revolution of 1979 that had toppled the incumbent pro-American government.

Officially, Iran were drawn as Team B and USA as Team A for that game. Protocol dictated that Team B would walk towards Team A and shake hands. Iran's Supreme Leader Khamenei, however, had given strict orders to his players that under no circumstances would they walk to the Americans to shake hands. The game hadn't even started and everyone was already on edge!

Iran and Iraq had recently ended a vicious war in the Middle East, so to make matters worse, a Saddam Hussein-backed terrorist organisation had bought 7,000 tickets to watch the game in Lyon. There was no threat of imminent violence at the game, but a lot of propaganda was to be expected from the stands, given the global audience on the game.

Tensions hadn't previously been higher before a game of World Cup football. Speculation was rife as to what would happen when the teams emerged. What happened shocked the world. The Iranians came out with flowers for the Americans - flowers which included white roses which is a symbol of peace in Iran.

The two teams embraced in a friendly hug for a photo opportunity and then set out to play a fast-paced game marked by a healthy rivalry. USA would go on to lose 2-1 to the Iranians, but something much bigger than the result was at stake that day.

The friendliness and camaraderie of the 22 players on the pitch showed that football could easily transcend politics.

It was a beautiful show of humanity, with American defender Jeff Agoos summing it up nicely after the game: "We did more in 90 minutes than the politicians did in 20 years"

# THE KNOWN DICTATOR STORY

The 1930s in Europe saw the rapid rise of three movements that combined and peaked in the 1938 World Cup: Fascism, propaganda and international football matches.

Going into the 1934 World Cup, Europe was gripped by pre-war tension. Extreme right groups were dominating the political scene. Adolf Hitler was the leader in Germany, and in Italy, host of the World Cup, Benito Mussolini was in charge.

These dictators were pioneers in using propaganda to control the masses, and there was no better way to influence the people, than with *the* world's working class sport: football.

Aware of the game's cross-national appeal, Mussolini is said to have imposed a set of laws for the Italian players that would have to be adhered to unless they wanted to face the firing squad.

One of the easy rules to follow was to do the one-hand-in-the-air Fascist salute before each game. It was said this was to show respect to 'Il Duce', but also to intimidate the opposition - much like the Maori Haka before New Zealand rugby games.

The other rule they had to abide by, which was considerably harder to maintain, was that they *had* to win the tournament. If they didn't they faced death.

Apparently Mussolini threatened the head coach and all his players before the tournament. It was *that* important to him to show to the world that fascism was the way forward, and there was no better way to do it than beating everyone on the world stage.

Luis Monti, the Argentine-Italian player, has the distinctive honour of being the only ever player to represent two different countries in two world cup finals.

He played the finals in Uruguay in 1930 (which he lost whilst representing Argentina) and in Italy 1934 (which he won whilst playing for Italy). Years later, he would sum up his situation nicely, and somewhat in jest, by saying:

"In 1930, in Uruguay, locals wanted to kill me if I won, and in Italy, four years later, they wanted to kill me if I lost"

The Italian players performed well in France 1938, despite performing in front of many exiled Italian fans who were repugned by their pre-match fascist salutes.

They went on to beat Hungary in the final and claim back-to-back world titles. It seemed Il Duce's threat paid off.

# THE LESS KNOWN AND MORE OBVIOUS DICTATOR STORY

Much like Europe in the 1930s, South America had a spate of nasty dictators rule its countries in the twentieth century.

In 1978, Argentina hosted the World Cup. At that time, the country was ruled by the dictator Jorge Videla, and his country was going to play the tournament by a slightly different set of rules.

Much like Mussolini before him, and knowing the eyes of the world would be on the tournament, he used the World Cup to clean up Argentina's tarnished image around the world - he knew he could only do this by having the team win the tournament. He also had a little accomplice in Peruvian dictator Francisco Morales Bermudez.

The first thing Videla did was to delay Argentina kick off times until *after* the games in the other group had finished. That way the Argentinians *always* knew going into a game what the best result would be for them.

Unluckily for Argentina, the way things transpired in that tournament meant that they needed to beat Peru by 4 goals.

Even if they knew what they had to do *beforehand*, it was a massive ask. Peru had a great team at the time, they had drawn nil-nil with eventual finalists The Netherlands, and been named as having the best midfield of the group stages.

Lo and behold, The Argentines beat Peru 6-0. A monumental thrashing that beggars belief. They then went on to beat The Netherlands 3-1 in the final and win the World Cup.

The stories that have emerged from that Peru vs Argentina game are ones that are doused in embarrassment. Players from both Argentina and Peru have gone on record to express shame for taking part in a game that was so clearly fixed.

There have been unconfirmed rumours of Argentina paying $250,000 to the Peruvians if they threw the game. These seem to carry some truth however, with some inexplicable actions from the Peruvian manager at the time, like starting Argentine-born goalkeeper Ramon Quiroga in goal (instead of his traditional number one)

In 2012, Peru senator and opposition leader in 1978, Genaro Ledesma, testified in court that the game had indeed been thrown by the Peruvians.

According to Ledesma, Argentina let Peruvian dissidents (who were a threat to the incumbent Peruvian government) into their country, only on the grounds that Peru would throw the game.

To this day, that match fixing scandal remains one of the most obvious and worst kept secrets in the game.

It also remains a mystery why, given the evidence, nothing has been done by the world's governing body to retrospectively fix the debacle.

# CHAPTER 9
## THE HEART WRENCHERS

# DEAD FOR 5 MINUTES

There is no doubt that football pulls at our heartstrings more so than any other sport. More often than not it brings us unimaginable highs. But every so often, as in life, the sport takes us through moments of deep sadness.

In June 2021, during a Euro 2020 game, Danish footballer Christian Eriksen was walking towards the byline for a throw-in to be taken when his legs stopped working.

He sluggishly collapsed on the floor without anybody around him. Every footballer on the pitch immediately knew this was serious.

It turned out it wasn't his legs that had stopped working - it was his heart that had stopped beating.

The referee quickly stopped the game and told the medics to rush in, Eriksen's teammate Simon Kjaer rushed to go to Eriksen's side. He saw him collapsed on the ground, and immediately pushed his tongue down and cleared his breathing pathway.

This action would prove decisive in saving Eriksen's life. As things continued getting worse, and the extent of what was unfolding was clear (Eriksen was not just unconscious, he was medically dead!), Kjaer administered life-saving CPR.

Kjaer then instructed his teammates to form a protective shield around Eriksen as the medics used defibrillators to get his heart back to pumping blood around his body.

His teammates were clearly shocked. Some of them in tears, others in prayers.

Kjaer embraced Eriksen's wife Sabrina, who had rushed from the stands in a Denmark shirt bearing her husband's surname, and also shielded her from the horror that was unfolding before the world's eyes.

After a lengthy period of time the medics managed to stabilise Eriksen. The whole of the football community stood united in solidarity for those few minutes. Minutes that seemed like hours.

That event showed even the most effervescent of football fans, that there *are* more important things in life than football - like life itself.

Eriksen went on to make a full recovery and (surprisingly) continue his football career at the highest level.

Incredibly, Denmark managed to continue that game after the incident and lost to Finland. The result didn't matter though. The only result that mattered that day was that a human life had been brought back from death.

# SHOT BECAUSE OF AN OWN GOAL

Pelé tipped Colombia to win the World Cup in 1994 - or to at least make it to the semi-final. Such was the form of a Colombian side boasting the most talented generation of football players the country had ever seen.

They had gone 26 games unbeaten going into the World Cup, beating Argentina 5-0 in Buenos Aires in qualifying, and only conceding two goals in the process.

This was largely due to Andres Escobar being at the heart of their defence. He was known as "The Gentleman" due to his disciplined and clean style of play.

Colombia were knocked out in the group stage, thanks in large part to a 2-1 loss against home side USA. In that game, as Escobar was trying to block a cross, he inadvertently put the ball in the back of his own net.

The pre-tournament favourites were out of the World Cup at the first hurdle, and they flew back to Colombia. A Colombia, which at the time, was going through a civil war and was riddled with drug violence and criminal activity.

9 days after scoring his own goal, and despite pleas from team members to keep a low profile, Escobar found himself sitting in a car, outside a nightclub, embroiled in a discussion about his own goal.

The discussion ended with 6 gun shots to his back and the whole nation of Colombia mourning one of their most gifted footballers.

The official investigation concluded that it was a disgruntled football fan that fired the shots (he got given 43 years behind bars but got off after 11 years on good behaviour).

The 'word on the street' is that a Drug Baron who lost millions on a bet in the game ordered the killing and then paid $3m to government prosecutors to let him off and incarcerate someone else for the crime.

On the day of Escobar's funeral, 120,000 people lined up the streets of Medellin to pay their last respects to "The Gentleman" of Colombian football.

# THE GAME OF THEIR LIVES

Another heart wrenching tale to come from Medellin happened in November 2016.

Brazilian side Chapecoense were flying to the Colombian city to play the first leg of the Copa Sudamericana final against Atletico Nacional. The South American equivalent of the Europa League.

For a club that was only founded in 1973, and had come from the lower divisions of Brazil only recently, it was a huge feat. The players were about to compete in the biggest game of their lives.

Unfortunately, the chartered plane they were flying in wasn't fuelled properly. A few kilometres before reaching the airport in Medellin, the plane ran out of fuel and crashed, killing 71 of the 77 people onboard. The whole Chapecoense squad bar three players were killed that day.

The tragedy led to Nacional awarding the Copa Sudamericana title to Chapecoense in an act of solidarity to their

Brazilian counterparts. Nacional, in return, were awarded the Conmebol Fair Play Award that season.

The outpouring of support for Chapecoense came from every corner of the footballing globe, with retired players like Ronalidnho, Eidur Gudjohnsen, and Juan Roman Riquelme all offering to come out of retirement to play for the decimated Brazilian club.

Chapecoense, buoyed by a flurry of on-loan players, managed to *just* avoid relegation that season, and despite going down to Serie B the following year, they managed to turn it around and are now playing in Brazil's premier division.

One of the surviving players, goalkeeper Jackson Follman had his leg amputated and retired from football. Centre back Neto made a full recovery and played until his retirement in 2019. Left Back Alan Ruschel is still plying his trade as a footballer in his native Brazil.

That footballing tragedy brought the world together. It was something that hadn't happened since the 1958 Busby Babes tragedy, when Manchester United suffered a similar accident on a snowy runway in Belgrade. (See chapter 7)

CHAPTER 10
# THE RECORD BREAKERS

# ZOMBIE FOOTBALLERS? THE WORLD'S LONGEST MATCH

This chapter pays homage to the remarkable events in football that have broken world records. And there's no better place to start than mentioning a feat that was achieved *purely* for the love of the game and, which in the end, helped a great cause.

In 2019 a group of amateur football players decided to break a record for the longest football game ever played.

To do this, they played continuously in a mind-numbing and strength-sapping football match that lasted 169 hours!

Don't even bother doing mental arithmetic. We'll save you the effort straight away. That's one week and 1 hour of continuous football.

Playing football is any fan's dream, but doing *anything* continuously for over a week would surely test your resolve.

Tempers frayed and tears were shed in the course of the marathon, as players stumbled on for hour after hour, day after day. But the play had to go on uninterrupted if they wanted to break the record.

The teams were aiming to beat the Guinness World record of 134 hours, but as they played, the distressing news came in that a German side had played for 168 hours. So, they played grimly onwards for the extra day and a half.

The scoreline ended up at 988-951, and luckily for everyone involved, it was safely beyond the need for a penalty shootout!

Cancer Research was the real winner at the end of the week, with the charity *Kicking Off Against Cancer* raising thousands of pounds through their efforts.

# EXTRA...EXTRA...EXTRA TIME!

Amateur footballers provided the longest football game on record, but it was at the Pirelli ground in Burton, England, that the record for the longest stoppage time ever added to a game of football was recorded.

Bournemouth were playing away to Burton in September 2019 when the floodlights at the ground failed. Not once, not twice, but a surprising three times.

The lights were out for a total of 28 minutes, but astonishingly, the game did not get called off. Instead the referee kept the clock ticking and simply added 28 minutes as stoppage time at the end of regulation time.

Luckily for Burton, it paved the way for a David-vs-Goliath victory over the Premier League side. They beat The Cherries 2-0 and it was not surprising that by the time the third outage came about, Bournemouth fans were already leaving the ground in disgust, and their players seemed discombobulated by the intermittent power failures.

Whether or not they were disorientated by the Pirelli Stadium blackouts, Bournemouth never saw that 2-0 defeat coming!

# BLINK AND YOU'LL MISS IT

The quickest goal ever recorded by the English Football Association was scored by Marc Burrows.

The English striker was playing for Cowes Sports Reserves against Eastleigh when, in 2004, he took a shot immediately after kick off.

Aided by some strong winds, the shot rocketed into the back of the opposition's net an impressive 2.56 seconds after kick off.

Nawaf Al Abed of Saudi Arabia claims to have scored in 2 seconds for Al Hilal against Al Shoalah, however his time has never been officially recorded by the Guiness Book of World Records.

There is little to no video evidence of the above two goals, so an honourable mention must go to Gavin Stokes of Maryhill FC, who wins the award of 'fastest-goal-where-there-is-plenty-of-video-evidence-for'.

After the Ballon D'or, that's the most coveted award in world football.

In 2017, Maryhill FC were facing Clydebank FC in a Scottish semi-professional league.

The Clydebank goalie was still adjusting his gloves when a looping shot straight from kick off by Stokes went past his head with only 3.2 seconds on the clock.

The fastest youth goal on record was delivered in a 2012 match in Serbia, when Dorkol's Vuk Bakic teed off to score a stunner against Polet. It stopped the clock at 2.2 seconds, beating Mark Burrows' previous record score for Cowes Sports Reserves against Eastleigh by a few seconds.

Bakic's goal is also very popular on YouTube and it makes for some great viewing for everyone – apart from the opposing goalkeeper.

# SARDINE SPECTATOR RECORD — MOST FANS IN A STADIUM

There is nothing quite like watching your favourite team play live. Perhaps an oddity, as the benefits of a comfy armchair, food, drink and live action replays ought to trump standing shoulder-to-shoulder with loud strangers.

Having said that, it's the atmosphere of a crowd that compels you to watch games live.

In 1923 Wembley Stadium hosted its first ever match: The FA Cup final between Bolton Wanderers and West Ham United.

The game drew a sell-out crowd of 126,000. However, about another 180,000 spectators fought their way into the stadium (much like some English fans did 100 years later for the Euro 2020 final!).

In the end, it is estimated that there were about 300,000 human beings packed inside Wembley Stadium that late April afternoon in 1923. (300,022 if you include the players on the pitch!)

The game had to be postponed for 45 minutes as the crowd spilled onto the playing field and rendered the pitch unplayable. That was easily fixed by the police though, who ingeniously (read: careless!) came round on horses and crammed the pitch invaders back into the stands.

Miraculously, nobody got trampled to death; and Bolton won their first ever FA Cup that day.

The official record for the most fans in one game, however, goes to the Maracana Stadium in Brazil.

Uruguay was being hosted by Brazil for the 1950 World Cup final. Interest was at fever pitch, resulting in 199,854 people clicking over the turnstiles!

That game went down in footballing folklore for many reasons (it's known as the "Maracanazo" around the world) not just because of the size of the crowd, but also because it was expected to be Brazil's first ever triumph on the world stage.

Twelve winners' medals had been made in advance and inscribed with the Brazilian team's names. The local press had even published a newspaper edition with the banner headline "Brazil: World Champions!!!"

Unfortunately for printers across Brazil, Uruguay went on to win 2-1. It's safe to say that the match also holds the record for the highest numbers of *sad* spectators leaving a stadium.

In the modern, safety-first grounds, the largest football crowd ever recorded was in the Michigan Stadium, USA, in 2014.

The super-sized American stadium filled up with about 109,000 spectators supporting Manchester United and Real Madrid, who were competing in the International Champions Cup. A big crowd for a friendly game.

# WHERE DID THAT ONE COME FROM?

Names that you associate with long range net busters may include your David Beckhams, Xabi Alonsos Wayne Rooneys etc.

But if you linger on the thought a little longer, it makes sense that the longest goals in world history have always come from goalkeepers. And, more often than not, they are completely accidental.

Asmir Begovic long held the crown for the longest goal in history (and incidentally, one of the quickest goals ever too!) when he netted after 13 seconds for Stoke City against Southampton in the English Premier League.

The Bosnian received a back pass soon after kick off, and under some pressure from the Southampton striker, decided to boot it up the field from 91.9 metres away.

Neither of the Southampton centre backs dealt with the looping ball, which went past them and bounced over a red-faced Southampton keeper.

As is often the case with these long-range efforts, it's the bounce of the ball that throws the opposing keepers off and sees them bashfully pick up the ball from their own net.

Begovic held the record for the longest goal until a goalkeeper that goes by the name of Tom King took one fateful goal kick in January 2021.

The Newport County goalkeeper saw his goal kick bounce on the edge of the opposition area and nestle itself into the top left hand corner of Cheltenham's goal.

A very subdued celebration followed - perhaps due to him being unaware that he, at 96.01 metres away from goal, had just scored the longest goal in football history!

He was also the only name on the scoresheet for Newport that day, a game that finished in a 1-1 draw.

It is increasingly likely that if that record is ever broken, it will have to come from somebody taking a shot from very near their own corner flag!

# GIANTS OF THE GAME

Football tends to be a sport for the quick and flexible, with height being a particular advantage for defenders and strikers.

The game nonetheless has had some behemoths on the pitch, men who in other circumstances would have been snapped up as props for their local rugby team.

Whilst some of them do well to keep the pounds in check whilst still playing football, they gain more notoriety after retirement due to their increase in weight.

Notable mentions include Ronaldo, Maradona, Mido who have all ballooned in weight after hanging up their boots.

However, the real heroes are the ones that produced world class performances despite their build.

Micky Quinn, born in 1962, was one of those players whose muscular frame eventually ran him into weight issues.

He was, however, a force to be reckoned with until his bulk slowed him down, scoring 227 goals in his 535-game professional career.

In his prime, at 88kg in weight, he was still doing the job with with fans cheering him on by singing —*He's fat, he's round, he scores at every ground, Micky Quinn, Micky Quinn.*

Opposing fans were less kind, but that did not stop him scoring goals.

Another player who combined a large size in suits with footballing talent was Kevin Pressman.

At 1.85m he could, and he *did* carry a lot of weight, 98 kilograms to be precise, constituting a *very* large presence in goal for his 500 games at Sheffield Wednesday.

One of the modern greats, great in size more than ability that is, is Adebayo Akinfenwa. Weighing in at 101kg, the charismatic Wycombe Wanderers player is somewhat of a celebrity in English circles for his post-match celebrations.

Because of his large stature, he is often the highest scoring player in the 'strength' category in football video games.

The King of Timber award in our list of football heavies goes to William Foulke.

Foulke filled the goalmouth at 1.9m and 150kg by the end of his professional career.

Foulke won a cap for England in 1897 and played most of his long career for Sheffield United. He truly was the monster of all monsters, yet surprisingly limber, despite his tonnage.

# FFS! RED CARD AT THE SPEED OF LIGHT...

In the year 2000, Lee Todd was red carded after 2 seconds whilst playing for Cross Farm Park Celtic.

The striker got his marching orders whilst his teammates roared with laughter. They all thought it was a joke.

It was not, and the bemused Sunday League player is now the unenviable record-holder for the fastest ejection from the field in the history of red cards!

As the players were getting ready for kick off, referee Peter Kearle let the Sunday League players know that he would NOT tolerate any swearing on the football pitch.

He proceeded to blow the whistle for kick off, and Todd, being a striker for Celtic, found himself right next to the referee when he blew.

Todd clapped his hands to his ears in pain and muttered "fuck me, ref, that was loud!"

The referee, true to his word, did not tolerate the colourful language and showed him a straight red.

Todd laughed. Everyone laughed. It was hilarious. Only the referee was not amused. Despite all that Todd or his teammates could do in appealing to common sense, the ref held firm.

The Green Stripes found themselves playing the next 89 minutes and 58 seconds of the game without their striker.

The rank injustice spurred Cross Farm Park Celtic to superhuman heights. They won the match 11-2, with Todd following on from the sideline.

Todd picked up a £27 profanity fine, along with a severe five-week ban.

There *was* a silver lining to the story, though. National TV picked up the incident as the "funny story" of the week-end, and Lee Todd got his face on telly where producers where at the ready to bleep out any foul language.

He has become a local legend, and the story is getting repeated down the generations. He still gets the occasional sympathy pint down the pub on account of his scrape with the football law, perhaps well worth a red card after all…

# THE GREATEST GOAL GULF
# OF ALL TIME

Fans of other sports may knock football because of its lack of 'points' or goals. If you ever have to find yourself defending the excitement of our beautiful game, then perhaps point those other sports fans to this chapter.

The biggest winning margin in a game of football was 149-0. It happened in a match played between AS Adema and SO l'Emyrne of Madagascar in 2002. *The Guinness Book of Records* has it down as the world's biggest ever loss, but it never really was a 'competition'.

SO l'Emyrne threw the game by deliberately scoring own goals for 90 minutes. This was in protest against a disputed refereeing decision in the previous week's game. The poor ref at that game was powerless, and had to keep on blowing for the goal and re-starting play. For a whole hour and a half.

The game was meant to be a mouth-watering showdown between two ancient rivals, so the spectators demanded their money back after the game.

The local football association banned the coach and the captain of SO l'Emyrne for the rest of the season, and both teams (unfairly for one) got a severe reprimand.

The biggest scoreline, from a match where two professional* teams were actually competing, was delivered by Arbroath FC of Scotland.

They buried the hapless Bon Accord FC under 36 goals in the 1885 Scottish Cup. Bon Accord might have been outgunned, but at least they honourably *tried* to play

In the modern era, though, the biggest drubbing on record happened in the South Pacific, when American Samoa lost their FIFA World Cup qualifier to Australia by 31-0 in 2002.

It was spectacular, but hardly a footballing spectacle. Australian Archie Thompson scored a world-record 13 goals in that match, but it's doubtful that that award is hung front and centre in his trophy cabinet.

*paid footballers didn't come until much later, but they were compensated in other ways

# BURY ME IN MY BOOTS —
# I'LL NEVER HANG THEM UP!

Many footballers love the game too much to stop playing at a reasonable age.

It is very common to see fifty-year olds routinely lumber over marshy club fields on Sunday afternoons, occasionally embarrassing younger, less skilled players with defence splitting passes. They are a fine body of footballers.

Still, nobody can hold a candle to Ezzeldin Bahader, the world's oldest professional football player who plays for Egyptian club October 6.

On March 7 2020, Bahader became the oldest active professional football player by coming onto the pitch at the grand old age 74 years and 125 days.

He missed a penalty in a 3-2 defeat to El Ayat Sports Club, while entering *The Guinness Book of Records*. He also dislodged a disgruntled Isaak Hayik, who at 73 had been the previous record holder.

The following year, at 75, Bahader pushed new boundaries by scoring a professional goal for October 6 playing in the derby match against El Alyat.

Despite dizziness and a wonky knee, Bahader emerged from Covid-19 lockdown to play a full 90 minutes, and this time scored from the spot.

Bahader might have retired from his job as a civil engineer, but his footballing career is still going strong at the time of writing.

With six grandchildren, he is never going to be short of supporters!

# MOST PENALTY MISSES IN ONE GAME

Martin Palermo holds one of those records no footballer wants to have, let alone an Argentinian footballer.

In 1999 he delivered a performance that defied all odds.

It was the group stages of the Copa America, and Argentina were favourites to beat Colombia and top their group.

What should have been a routine win for La Albiceleste started going ominously wrong after just five minutes.

A Colombian defender handled the ball in the box, and, as the assigned penalty expert, Palermo confidently stepped up to the spot. He slammed an unstoppable missile into the crossbar— making the ball bounce away into the stands.

It was early. There was plenty of time for it to get worse for Palermo.

With Colombia taking the lead via a penalty kick (Ivan Ramiro Cordoba showing Martin Palermo how to do it),

Argentina got awarded yet another penalty kick. Funnily enough the same defender handled the ball in the area *again*!

Redemption time!

Palermo stepped up and spun the ball into place on the spot. He walked back about half a kilometre, sprinted in and…fired the ball over the crossbar.

The fans were not amused. The management were not amused. Colombians were all in stitches! The Argentinian coach, Bielsa, ran onto the field in an apoplectic rage at Palermo, and got red-carded.

In stoppage time Colombia were leading 3-0. The game was well and truly finished, so when Palermo got fouled in the Colombian penalty area and won a penalty kick, he quickly dusted himself off, grabbed the football and placed it on the spot.

Surely that was the only thing the Argentinians would rescue from the match. Palermo had the chance to atone his two previous penalty misses.

So with arguably the most important thing to play for in his career, his dignity, he took a couple of steps back and took the penalty.

The goalkeeper, Miguel Calero, guessed the direction of the kick and the ball went straight into the midriff of the goalkeeper, who joined in the Colombian celebrations after the full time whistle went shortly after.

Palermo dropped out of the international football scene in what can only be described as a blaze of ignominy. He is the only holder of this "anti-hat trick" in football, a record three penalties fluffed in an international encounter.

# RED CARD FOR THE REF

Referee Graham Poll delivered a shocker of a performance in 2006. So much so that it ended his international whistle-blowing career.

Croatia and Australia met at the World Cup in Germany both needing to win the fixture to progress to the second round.

Poll, in fairness to him, blew an impeccable first half. It was Poll's second half that left a lot to be desired!

In the 61st minute of the game, Croatian defender, Josip Šimunić, was yellow carded for bringing Harry Kewell down in the edge of the box.

Kewell then equalised for the Aussies to make it 2-2. The final few minutes turned out to be a nail-biting spectacle as the players were trying *desperately* to win the game. In their desperation, both teams had a man sent off.

At two-all and ten a side, things were getting breathless. Just before stoppage time, Šimunić knocked down an Australian attacker in the area. Poll blew for the penalty and awarded Šimunić another yellow card.

The world stood still, waiting for Poll to show Šimunić the mandatory red that follows two yellow cards… only that never happened!

Poll *forgot* that Šimunić had been previously booked and failed to send him off. Play continued.

After the game, the referee admitted that he had written the previous yellow card under another player's number in his book, and that's why the second yellow never turned into a red.

As soon as Šimunić realised his luck, you would have thought that he would hide himself away on the field somewhere.

Quite the opposite happened. Šimunić wasn't very good at hiding himself away on the field, and in the 93rd minute, with justice prevailing (or stupidity prevailing, it depends on who you ask), Šimunić got booked for the third time for *dissent*. Imagine riding your luck that badly that you show dissent *after* having already been booked twice!

Third time *was* the charm for Poll, and he rightfully remembered to send the player off.

The game ended 2-2 and Poll got sent home by tournament officials the next day. That costly error led to his retirement from international football.

Šimunić is still probably arguing somewhere against that sending off.

# THE LONGEST PENALTY SHOOT-OUT EVER

Liverpool and Middlesbrough hold third place for the longest shootout ever. It was in a 2014 third round play-off in the Capital One Cup. Scores were level after full-time and when they went to penalties, they had to cycle through their entire team and start from the beginning *again* before Liverpool won 14-13 on penalties.

Athens lost 14-15 to Olympiakos in the 2009 Greek Cup Final to claim stake to the second longest ever penalty shootout. It equaled Brockenhurst and Andover Town's epic shootout on a misty October evening in 2013.

What was special about Brockenhurst and Andover, though, was that every single shot went in, except the last one, giving Brockenhurst the win! By contrast, Athens and Olympiakos had to blast, slice, hook and bump a total of 34 kicks towards goal.

The two goalkeepers managed to block five shots on the way to the final result. That means they had to cycle through all their players *three times* before the winner could emerge!

That is, however, nothing compared to KK Palace and Civics, the two teams that were in the final of the 2005 Namibian Cup, and rightful holders of the longest ever penalty shootout.

They had to cycle through their entire team *four times* before KK Civics emerged as victors 17-16 on penalties!

A shout out to the French Cup sides Obernai and Wittelsheim, who slugged it out, goal for goal in the deepening dusk, until the kickers couldn't see the goal and the goalie couldn't see the kickers.

It was 1996 and they did not yet have pitch lighting. Just like a county cricket match, they called the game off for bad lighting after they were tied 15-15 on penalties.

The local FA granted Obernai a bye to the next round on the basis that they were the lower-ranked team. Slightly outrageous if you were a Wittelsheim fan.

# TEMPORARY MANAGER — SHORTEST TIME ON THE JOB

In 2007, Leroy Rosenior had ten minutes to spare, so he used them to manage Torquay United.

The chairman of the board, Mike Bateson, signed Rosenior as manager, and immediately after, sold 51% of the club to a consortium bidder.

Rosenior quickly realised that it meant the new owners were free to choose whatever manager they might want. Which effectively terminated his employment in a breathtaking ten minutes!

This led to a bit of scrap in the club. Not the ones they were used to in the goalmouths of their own area, but one in the legal area and one which involved lawyers and barristers.

The club had just been relegated to the third division, and Bateson thought Rosenior was the man to get them out of the crisis. The new owners, however, disagreed.

Words were spoken and Rosenior got the boot, verbally. But not contractually. This was a classic boardroom shambles. Rosenior stayed on as caretaker manager until the next manager took over in June, but officially, his dates of holding office are recorded as 17 May 2007—17 May 2007.

By contrast, the second shortest tenure as manager of a football club allowed Crystal Palace's Dave Bassett to impart much more of his philosophy to the team.

His tenure of the club in 1984 lasted for a lengthy four days.

# THE INVINCIBLES

In 2004 Arsenal achieved a feat that had only ever been achieved *once* before in English Top Flight football. And it's a feat that has never before been seen in modern English football: They went a *whole* season without being defeated.

The only other team to have done it was Preston North End. But they did it in the 1888-1889 season, when it can be argued that it was an easier feat to achieve.

On the back of their unbeaten status, Arsene Wenger's boys won the Premier League in 2004 with 26 wins and a modest (although still impressive) 90 points.

As a result of that magic season, Gunners' fans often reminisce about The Invincibles, although they have not been able to reproduce their glory days since then.

That memorable season saw Thierry Henry lead the way in attack with 30 goals, which ended up being an impressive proportion of the Gunner's total of 73 goals. Arsenal graced the league in the early noughties with the most exhilarating display of attackers which included Robert Pires, Freddy Ljunberg and Dennis Bergkamp.

Many note, though, that the defence played a huge role. Led by goalkeeper Jens Lehmann, the back line limited the opposition teams to a miserly 26 goals that season.

The truth is that The Invincibles were unbeatable simply because they had all round quality all over the pitch.

Arsenal went on to lift a special one-off golden edition of the Premier League trophy that season.

## TOP INTERNATIONAL GOAL SCORER — RONALDO

Strikers come in all different shapes and sizes. Some are left-footed and some are right-footed. Some are ambipedal, and some are great with their head.

For all strikers though, it's all a numbers game, and the man with the biggest number is Cristiano Ronaldo.

At the time of writing, he has netted 117 goals in 189 matches for Portugal – and he is still going strong!

He has also netted when it matters. A 'big game' player so to speak. Memorable goals include an outrageous bicycle kick in the Champions League final against Juventus and a headed goal against Sampdoria in which we jumped so high (2.56 metres in the air!) that his feet were above the defender marking him!

His ability makes him one of the most heavily-decorated football players. He's won five *Ballons d'Or* for FIFA's Player of the Year, and four Golden Boots as leading goal scorer amongst top-tier European players.

He has also won a dozen assorted league medals, and has 5 European Cups wins to his name. He also led Portugal to victory in the European Championships and the Nation's League in 2019.

The man quite simply is a phenomenon. Although "The Phenomenon" is the nickname of the other great football player called Ronaldo, so to avoid confusion, let's not go there…

# NET-BUSTER EXTRAORDINAIRE — LIONEL MESSI

The Ronaldo vs Messi debate is one that will rage in football chats across the world for years to come. So in the interest of fairness, it's only right that we talk about the other world great.

Messi has won the Ballon D'or a record 7 times. The Ballon D'or is voted by football journalists and international football coaches and captains. So when your fellow professionals award you with the prize, you know you're doing a good job. Especially when you compete in an era with no other than Cristiano Ronaldo.

The Argentina striker has continuously amassed hundreds of goals. Especially in the prime of his career whilst playing for Barcelona.

However it was in 2012, that he blew every competitor out of the water with a benchmark bomb.

In a single calendar season he amassed 91 goals! Ninety-one! *Noventa y uno!*

That was 79 for Barcelona and 12 for Argentina. A feat, that in all likelihood will never be equaled. As a matter of fact, the only player to perhaps coming close to beating that figure is… well, himself!

It is only apt to finish the book by paying homage to the best two football players of the 21st century.

Whether you think one player is better than the other, what we can all agree on is that because of them, the sport has benefited.

And when they sport benefits, *we* are the real winners.

# CHAPTER 11
## A QUICK FAVOUR

Reviews are the bedrock of my success. Taking 5 minutes of your time to review this book will benefit me in one of two ways. If the book wasn't to your satisfaction, please leave constructive criticism to make me a better author. If you enjoyed the book, a good review will give my book more clout in the Amazon algorithms and generate more exposure for my books. I'd be extremely grateful if you could rate my book now. Thank you.

Instagram: @itsmikelangdon

# CHAPTER 12
# **REFERENCES**

Ashdown, J. (2008, September 21). *Phantom goal will haunt rookie referee | Watford.* The Guardian. https://www.theguardian.com/football/2008/sep/22/watford.reading

Bailey, R. (2014). *The 10 Worst Ever Football Debuts | News, Scores, Highlights, Stats, and Rumors.* Bleacher Report. https://bleacherreport.com/articles/2161645-the-10-worst-ever-football-debuts

BBC News. (2022, March 17). *Emiliano Sala: Footballer died after plane broke up mid-air.* BBC. https://www.bbc.com/news/uk-wales-60767283

BBC Sport. (2017). *Maryhill's Gavin Stokes scores 3.2 seconds after kick-off.* BBC. https://www.bbc.com/sport/av/rugby-union/39580244

Bollons, M. (2016, March 30). *Liverpool's Champions League Final Comeback Against AC Milan Still Baffles Kaka.* Bleacher Report. https://bleacherreport.com/articles/2628815-liverpools-champions-league-final-come-back-against-ac-milan-still-baffles-kaka

Catley, N. (2022, April 20). *Memories of Reading's ghost goal at Watford.* Watford Observer. https://www.watfordobserver.co.uk/sport/20080205.memories-readings-ghost-goal-watford/

Clarkson, R. (2022). *Articles > The biggest football attendances ever recorded.* Football Ground Map. https://www.footballgroundmap.com/articles/the-biggest-football-attendances-ever-recorded

Craigie, E. (2021, March 13). *Heathrow: how Albanian national football team nearly took £2,500 of duty free without paying.* Berkshire Live. https://www.getreading.co.uk/news/berkshire-history/heathrow-how-albanians-national-football-19978286

Dawkes, P., & Holyman, I. (2020, May 7). *Calais Racing Union: The amateur team that went to Coupe de France final.* BBC. https://www.bbc.co.uk/sport/football/52553649

de Menezes, J. (2016). *71 People Die in Plane Crash Involving Brazilian Football Team Chapecoense.* Bleacher Report. https://bleacherreport.com/articles/2678766-plane-carrying-brazilian-soccer-club-crashes-in-colombia

Disquss. (2021, February 1). *What is the longest goal ever scored in football history & who holds the record?* Goal.com. https://www.goal.com/en-om/news/what-is-the-longest-goal-ever-scored-football-history-who/1c602omv2jymaz94izgx6m2un

Doe, L. (2013, February 1). *Football's Believe it or not: 10 most bizarre but true stories*. Sportslens.com. https://sportslens.com/news/ten-bizarre-football-stories/

Dove, E. (2020, October 19). *74-year-old Egyptian grandfather becomes the world's oldest footballer*. Goal.com. https://www.goal.com/en/news/74-year-old-egyptian-grandpa-becomes-the-worlds-oldest/1oerfpbxr1pkr11fw-pddjs644a

Downes, W., Gordon, J., Gannon, T., Newsham, G., Shilton, A., Hutchinson, J., Watson, J., & Gysin, P. (2018, May 10). *England hero Gary Lineker talks about the infamous moment he pooed himself at Italia '90 World Cup*. The Sun. https://www.thesun.co.uk/sport/football/6252441/england-gary-lineker-toilet-pants-poo/

Erel, F. (2019, February 8). *Tragedy in air: Footballers who died in plane crashes*. Anadolu Agency. https://www.aa.com.tr/en/sports/tragedy-in-air-footballers-who-died-in-plane-crashes/1387468#

Flynn, E. (2019, July 4). *The imperfect hat-trick: Martin Palermo's three missed penalties – and so much more – 20 years on*. FourFourTwo. https://www.fourfourtwo.com/features/martin-palermo-three-missed-penalties-argentina-colombia-1999-copa-america

Footy Fair. (2014). *Hammer for a Day: The Unlikely Story of Steve Davies*. FOOTY FAIR. http://www.footyfair.com/2015/07/hammer-for-day-unlikely-story-of-steve.html

Furniss, M. (2022, July 8). *About That Game: Brazil 1-7 Germany (2014)*. The Analyst. https://theanalyst.com/2022/07/brazil-1-7-germany-stats-story/

Guardian Unlimited Staff. (2007, May 21). *Leroy Rose-nior's 10 minute stint at Torquay Utd is shortest manage-rial reign in English football*. The Guardian. https://www.theguardian.com/football

/2007/may/21/newsstory.sport5

Healy, J. (2020, November 25). *How Diego Maradona used the Hand of God to claim revenge for a bloody conflict between Britain and Argentina.* ABC. https://www.abc.net.au/news/2020-11-26/diego-maradona-hand-of-god-1986-world-cup-quarter-final/12922018

Ingle, S. (2006). Cambridge Dictionary | English Dictionary, Translations & Thesaurus. https://www.theguardian.com/football/worldcup2006blog/2006

/jun/15/urbanmyths1truth0#comment-276772

Jones, M. (2014). *Football's 7 Greatest Cinderella Stories of All Time | News, Scores, Highlights, Stats, and Rumors.* Bleacher Report. https://bleacherreport.com/articles/1924032-footballs-7-greatest-cinderella-stories-of-all-time

Jorden, A. (2009). *"The Treble Looms Large!" A Look Back at the 1999 Man Utd Treble.* Bleacher Report. https://bleacherreport.com/articles/161417-the-treble-looms-large-a-lookback-at-the-1999-man-utd-treble

Kenmare, J. (2021, October 31). *It's Been 21 Years Since The Fastest Red Card In Football History And We Found The Man Responsible.* SPORTbible. https://www.sport-bible.com/football/news-legends-exclusives-its-been-21-

years-since-the-fastest-red-card-in-football-history-20211031

Maysh, J. (2013, September 5). *The day Harry Redknapp brought a fan on to play for West Ham.* The Guardian. https://www.theguardian.com/football/blog/2013/sep/05/harry-redknapp-played-fan-west-ham

McKenzie, C., & Shoker, S. (2016, April 30). *Leicester City: The Premier League fairy tale gripping a city.* BBC. https://www.bbc.co.uk/news/uk-england-leicestershire-36160621

Miller, N. (2018, March 27). *World Cup stunning moments: Luis Suárez bites Giorgio Chiellini in 2014 | Nick Miller.* The Guardian. https://www.theguardian.com/football/blog/2018/mar/27/world-cup-stunning-moments-luis-suarez-bites-giorgio-chiellini-in-2014

Murphy, N. (2021, May 27). *Football's 5 longest penalty shootouts as Villarreal beat Man Utd in 11-10 epic.* Daily Star. https://www.dailystar.co.uk/sport/football/man-utd-longest-penalty-shootouts-24196918

Namunwa, K. (2019, September 26). *28 Minutes Makes Record For Longest Stoppage Time in Football.* Business Today Kenya. https://businesstoday.co.ke/28-minutes-stoppage-time-in-carabao-cup-breaks-football-record/

Onfido. (2022). *The strange case of Ali Dia: football's most famous fraudster.* Onfido. https://onfido.com/resources/gaming/the-strange-case-of-ali-dia-football-s-most-famous-fraudster

Parkinson, G. (2021, June 26). *The 10 all-time men's international top scorers*. FourFourTwo. https://www.four-fourtwo.com/features/highest-international-football-goalscorers-all-time-cristiano-ronaldo-portugal

Passmore, M. (2019, July 22). *KICKING OFF AGAINST CANCER: 169 HOURS OF FOOTBALL | News*. Cardiff City House of Sport. https://www.cardiffcityhouseofsport.-co.uk/news/kicking-off-against-cancer-world-record-attempt/

Pearce, S. (2018, October 29). *5 Urban Myths in Football That Just Aren't True*. 90min. https://www.90min.-com/posts/6209500-5-urban-myths-in-football-that-just-aren-t-true

Planet Football. (2021, December 22). *The players with the most goals in a calendar year: Messi, Ronaldo...* Planet Football. https://www.planetfootball.com/quick-reads/the-players-with-the-most-goals-in-a-calendar-year-messi-ronaldo/

Platt, O. (2021). *Arsenal Invincibles: How Wenger's 2003-04 Gunners went a season without defeat*. Goal.com. https://www.goal.com/en-gb/news/arsenal-invincibles-how-wengers-2003-04-gunners-went-a/1xkm3tgyvsb-jj1wzrewhqz0liu

Rosengarten, J. (2021, June 6). *How Denmark won Euro '92 without qualifying*. Optus Sport. https://sport.optus.-com.au/articles/os26723/the-incredible-story-of-how-denmark-won-euro-92-without-qualifying

Roy, R. (2019, February 14). *The Munich Air Disaster and The Busby Babes - Last Word on Football*. Last Word on

Sports. https://lastwordonsports.com/football/2019/02/14/the-munich-air-disaster-and-busby-babes/

Sharp, W. (2018, June 15). *Three yellow cards and one red face: Graham Poll's World Cup nightmare of 2006.* These Football Times. https://thesefootballtimes.co/2018/06/15/three-yellow-cards-and-one-red-face-graham-polls-world-cup-nightmare-of-2006/

Sports Now. (2011, July 19). *Did India withdraw from the 1950 World Cup because they were not allowed to play barefoot?* Los Angeles Times. https://www.latimes.com/archives/blogs/sports-now/story/2011-07-19/did-india-withdraw-from-the-1950-world-cup-because-they-were-not-allowed-to-play-barefoot

Stevens, R. (2016, March 26). *How Pickles the dog found the World Cup trophy - 50 years on.* BBC. https://www.bbc.co.uk/sport/football/35872662

Sunday World Sport. (2022, May 12). *How it unfolded: Manchester City's remarkable last-gasp win over QPR in 2012.* Sunday World. https://www.sundayworld.com/sport/soccer/how-it-unfolded-manchester-citys-remarkable-last-gasp-win-over-qpr-in-2012/41642381.html

Tendulkar, S. (2022, May 15). *WATCH: When Andrew Symonds took 'law into hands' and tackled a streaker during Aus vs Ind match in 2008.* Times Now. https://www.timesnownews.com/sports/cricket/took-law-into-my-own-hands-when-symonds-opened-up-on-infamous-streaker-incident-during-aus-vs-ind-match-watch-article-91574786

The Guardian. (2015, September 29). *Referee pulls out gun during Brazilian football match – video*. The Guardian. https://www.theguardian.com/sport/video/2015/sep/29/referee-pulls-out-gun-during-brazilian-football-match-video

The Guardian Knowledge. (2013, July 2). *Football's boozy bonuses | Soccer*. The Guardian. https://www.theguardian.com/football/2013/jul/03/the-knowledge-football-boozy-bonus

Tompkins, M. (2021, March 31). *The Miraculous 'Cinderella Story' of When Greece Won Euro 2004 - ULTRA UTD*. This is Ultra UTD! https://ultrautd.com/when-greece-won-euro-2004/

T S Staff. (2015, November 28). *Top 20 Fattest Soccer Players of All Time*. TheSportster. https://www.thesportster.com/soccer/top-20-fattest-soccer-players-of-all-time/2/

Wikipedia. (2022). *AS Adema 149–0 SO l'Emyrne*. Wikipedia. https://en.wikipedia.org/wiki/AS_Adema_149%E2%80%930_SO_l%27Emyrne

Wikipedia. (2022). *Australia 31–0 American Samoa*. Wikipedia. https://en.wikipedia.org/wiki/Australia_31%E2%80%930_American_Samoa

Wikipedia. (2022). *Game of three halves*. Wikipedia. https://en.wikipedia.org/wiki/Game_of_three_halves

Wikipedia. (2022). *Lisbon Lions*. Wikipedia. https://en.wikipedia.org/wiki/Lisbon_Lions

Wikipedia. (2022). *1968 European Cup Final*. Wikipedia. https://en.wikipedia.org/wiki/1968_European_Cup_Final

Wilks, M. (2021, May 28). *The greatest centre back partnerships of all time.* 90min. https://www.90min.com/posts/greatest-centre-back-partnerships-all-time

Wilks, M. (2021, June 25). *The greatest strike partnerships of all time - ranked.* 90min. https://www.90min.com/posts/greatest-strike-partnerships-of-all-time-ranked

Worswick, C. (2020, May 28). *Bobby Moore and the mystery of the missing Bogotá bracelet.* The Guardian. https://www.theguardian.com/football/2020/may/28/bobby-moore-and-the-mystery-of-the-missing-bogota-bracelet

Wright, C. (2013, September 17). *Classic Moments: Chris Nicholl Scores All Four Goals In Aston Villa's 2-2 Draw With Leicester City, 1976.* Who Ate all the Pies. https://www.whoateallthepies.tv/aston_villa/175548/classic-moments-chris-nicholl-scores-all-four-goals-in-aston-villas-2-2-draw-with-leicester-city-1976.html

Glendenning, B. (2018, April 3) World Cup stunning moments: Andres Escobar's deadly own goal. The Guardian.

https://www.theguardian.com/football/blog/2014/mar/25/world-cup-moments-andres-escobar-death

Roper, M. (2012, February 9) We fixed it! Peru Senator claims 1978 World Cup game against Argentina was rigged. The Daily Mail https://www.dailymail.co.uk/sport/football/article-2098970/Argentina-cheated-World-Cup-1978-says-Peru-senator.html

Billigham, N. (2022, April 01) The most politically charged game in World Cup history. Four Four Two.

https://www.fourfourtwo.com/features/usa-vs-iran-france-98-most-politically-charged-game-world-cup-history

Fuentes, H. (2018, July 4) Los 20 mitos mas famosos e increibles en la historia de los mundiales de futbol. Guioteca.

https://www.guioteca.com/mitos-y-enigmas/los-20-mitos-mas-famosos-e-increibles-en-la-historia-de-los-mundiales-de-futbol-i/

Carruthers, E. (2022, March 18) Most bizarre red card? Argentine footballer sent off for falling on opponent. Givemesport.

https://www.givemesport.com/87985552-red-card-argentine-player-sent-off-for-falling-on-opponent-after-being-smashed-in-the-face-with-ball

McGarry, J (2022, July 8) Patrick Battison has barely recovered from his crunching tackle with Harald Schumacher 40 years on from the World Cup's most vicious foul. The Mail Online.

https://www.dailymail.co.uk/sport/football/article-10995761/Patrick-Battiston-barely-recovered-40-years-World-Cup-clash-Schumacher.html

. . .

Krishnan, J. (2021, May 7) Inside Lasagne-gate: Tottenham's food poisoning nightmare which handed Arsenal top four. The Mirror.

https://www.mirror.co.uk/sport/football/lasagnegate-tottenham-arsenal-food-poisoning-24061126


Hall, D. (2021, June 29) LUCKY STRIKE England Euro 2020 football team's bizarre superstitions and rituals from Kane's shaving to Walker's rotten shin pads. The Sun.

https://www.thesun.co.uk/sport/15428342/england-football-players-superstitions-pre-match-rituals/


Hytner, D. (2009, February 26). Superstitious mind leaves Touré red-faced over his yellow card. The Guardian.

https://www.theguardian.com/football/2009/feb/26/champions-league-arsenal-roma


Miller, N. (2018, March 27) World Cup stunning moments: Luis Suárez bites Giorgio Chiellini in 2014. The Guardian.

https://www.theguardian.com/football/blog/2018/mar/27/world-cup-stunning-moments-luis-suarez-bites-giorgio-chiellini-in-2014

Tejwani, K. (2021 February 15) Kevin Prince and Jerome Boateng: The Brothers who faced off in the World Cup. These Football Times.

https://thesefootballtimes.co/2021/02/15/kevin-prince-and-jerome-boateng-the-brothers-who-faced-off-in-the-world-cup/#:~:text=the%20World%20Cup-,Kevin%2DPrince%20and%20J%C3%A9r%C3%B4me%20Boateng%3A%20the%20brothers%20who%20faced,off%20in%20the%20World%20Cup&text=On%2023%20June%202010,event%20in%20World%20Cup%20history.


Anonymous. (2021, November 1) Historias insolitas de futbol: increibles hazanas arbitrales. Semana.

https://www.semana.com/cultura/libros/articulo/historias-insolitas-de-futbol-increibles-hazanas-arbitrales/202144/


Anonymous (2022, June 26) The worst transfers in football history - ranked.

90 Minutes. https://www.90min.com/posts/transfers-worst-signings-football-history-hazard-coutinho-dembele


Rollings, G. (2019, April 8) MY FATHER'S KEEPER Bert Trautmann's jaw-dropping story from Hitler Youth to heroic goalkeeper who won the FA Cup with a broken neck. The Sun.

https://www.thesun.co.uk/sport/8815402/bert-trautmann-the-keeper-hitler-youth-broken-neck/

.   .   .

Ellis, T. (2017 May 16) 11 footballers who played through the pain barrier (and definitely, definitely shouldn't have). Four Four Two.

https://www.fourfourtwo.com/features/11-footballers-who-played-through-pain-barrier-and-definitely-definitely-shouldnt-have

Staff, T. (2015, May 14) Top 10 Strangest football stories of all time. The Sportster.

https://www.thesportster.com/soccer/top-10-strangest-football-stories-of-all-time/

Smart, R. (2022, January 23) The crazy football match that saw an incredible 36 red cards shown. Sporf.

https://www.sporf.com/the-crazy-football-match-that-saw-an-incredible-36-red-cards-shown/

McKenzie, C. & Shoker, S. Leicester City: The Premier League Fairy Tale Gripping a City. BBC News.

https://www.bbc.co.uk/news/uk-england-leicestershire-36160621

.   .   .

Davis, M. (2014, August 28). When Manchester United signed a player for two freezers full of ice cream. Manchester Evening News.

https://www.manchestereveningnews.co.uk/in-your-area/manchester-united-signed-player-two-7683813


Anonymous (2020, April 14)Manchester United's grey kit: Gary Neville reflects on 1996 defeat at Southampton. Sky Sports.

https://www.skysports.com/football/news/11095/11972605/manchester-uniteds-grey-kit-gary-neville-reflects-on-1996-defeat-at-southampton


Newsham, G. (2018, April 30) LITTLE BIRD Garrincha: The bent-legged Brazilian genius was as famous for his football skills as he was for his love of women and booze. The Sun.

https://www.thesun.co.uk/sport/football/6157082/garrincha-the-bent-legged-brazilian-genius-was-as-famous-for-his-football-skills-as-he-was-for-his-love-of-women-and-booze/


Marquez, C. (unknown) Winston Coe, El arquero manco. Colgados Por el Futbol.

https://colgadosporelfutbol.com/winston-coe-el-arquero-manco/

.   .   .

Beech, R. (2013, September 10) Dog scores a great goal at the far post and runs off to celebrate. The Mirror.

https://www.mirror.co.uk/sport/football/news/dog-scores-great-goal-far-2263585

Unknown (1999, October 1) Seagull's goal gets nod from FA Chiefs. Reuters - IOL.

https://www.iol.co.za/sport/seagulls-goal-gets-nod-from-fa-chiefs-14752

Keith, F. (2022, June 24) Referee ruled out goal after his false teeth fell out as he tried blowing for full-time. Daily Star.

https://www.dailystar.co.uk/sport/football/referee-false-teeth-blowing-whistle-27316198

Printed in Great Britain
by Amazon